Vanuatu
The Foreign Education of Abel

Karin Jensen & Abel Nako

Karin Jensen and Abel Nako

VANUATU
The Foreign Education of Abel

A dramatized biography

When we travel, it is we who are the strangers.
An invitation to travel responsibly.

VANUATU: The Foreign Education of Abel
Copyright © 2019 by Karin Jensen
Maps by Google Maps

ReadToDiscover.com
Building Cultural Bridges

ISBN 978-1-950724-33-8

South Pacific Island, Indigenous Cultures, Cultural Heritage, Land diving, Education, Family Values, Black Magic

CONTENTS

Chapter 1   Life is Good

Chapter 2   Village Education

Chapter 3   Christmas Celebrations

Chapter 4   Initiation Ceremony

Chapter 5   Yield or Resist

Chapter 6   Adapt or Perish

Chapter 7   Rough Beginnings

Chapter 8   The Hunt

Chapter 9   Black Magic

Chapter 10   Other Lands, Other Customs

Chapter 11   Studies

Chapter 12   Returning Home

Chapter 13   Tradition Meets Change

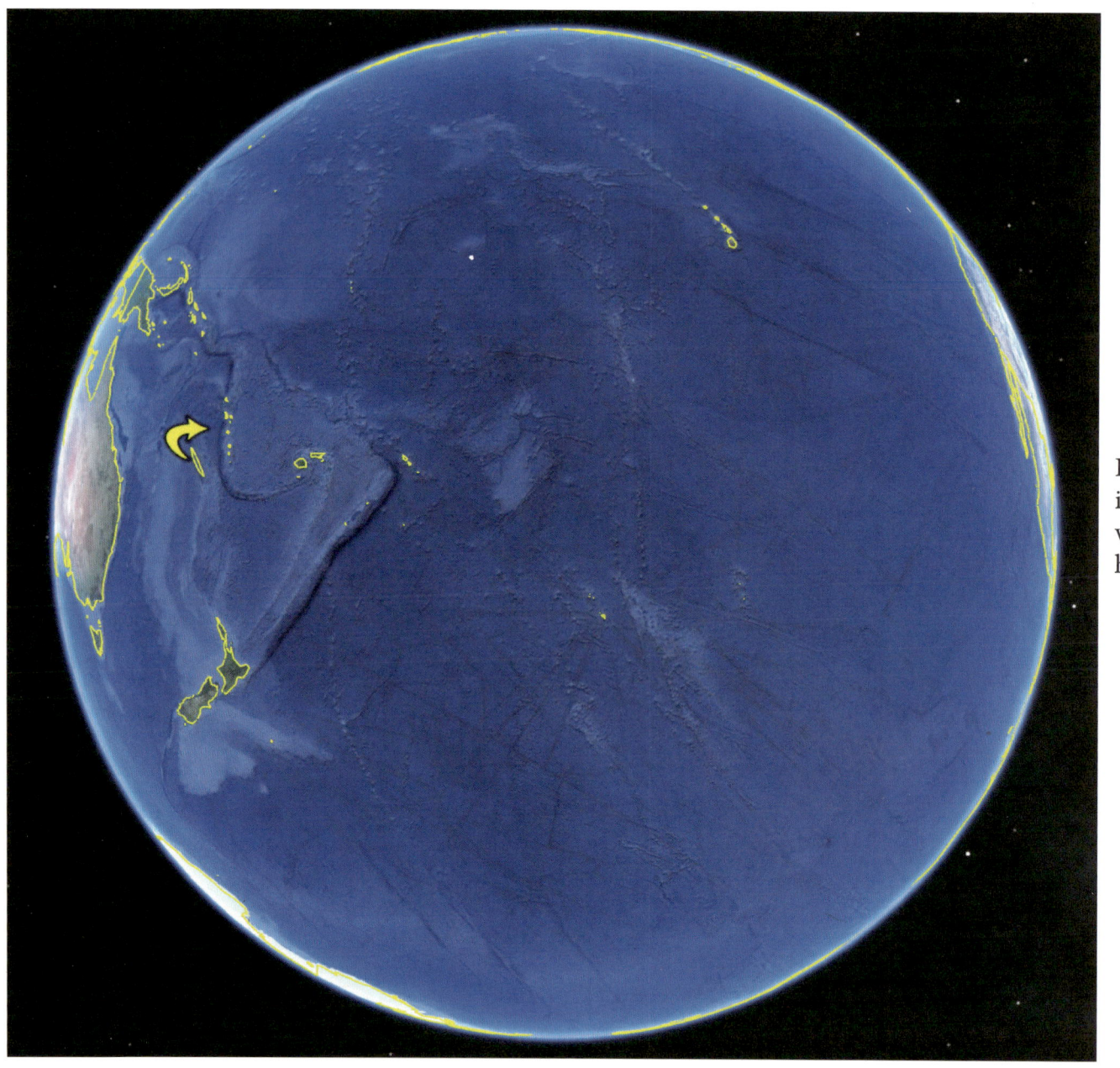

In the vast Pacific Ocean there is an archipelago of about 80 volcanic islands. Since 1980 it has been called Vanuatu

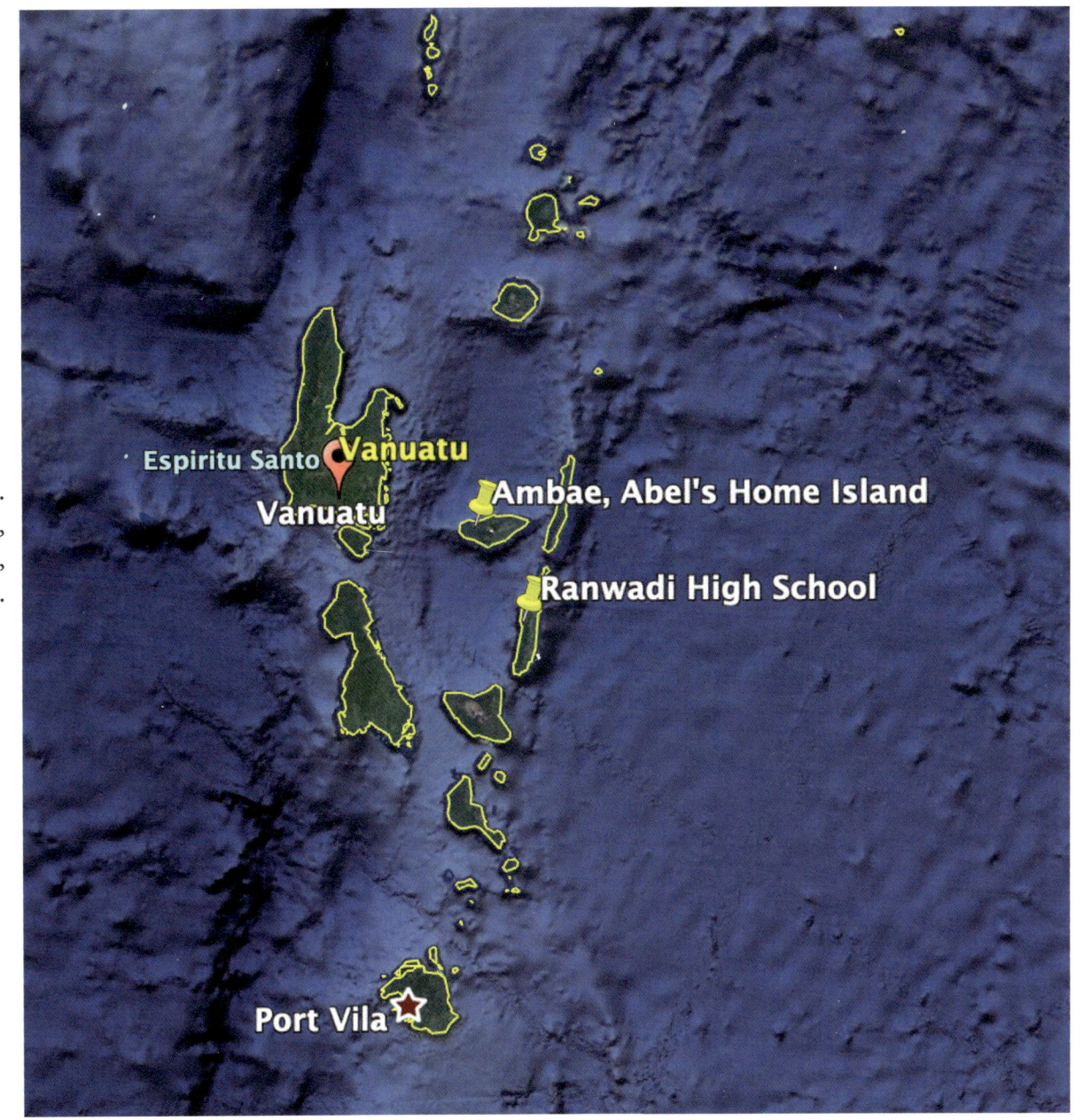

Abel lives on the island of Ambae. Ranwadi High, his new school, is situated on Pentecost Island, 90 nautical miles from his home.

Chapter 1: Life is Good

From my perch in the crown of our coconut palm, I look out over the entire world I know. With each swing of the machete, a ripe coconut hits the ground with a satisfying thud. I smile. Beneath my feet lies our vegetable patch, where taro and kumara are ripe for the harvest. Further down the mountain, the thatched roofs of our village are surrounded by the jungle, alive with birds and bats and myriads of creatures. And beyond the forest, out in the ocean, Uncle Toa and other fishermen are bobbing on the waves in their canoes, catching fish for our dinner.

The rainy season has started, as it always does, at the end of November, bringing with it regular downpours and higher temperatures. Right now, though, a light breeze dries the sweat on my neck. I would stay up here all day if Bumbu Joshua weren't waiting for me down in our vegetable patch.

Up here, so close to heaven, all my worries seem far away. Just this morning, my brother Dura snatched the last wing of the roasted fruit bat out of my hand and ate it. If he walked by right now, I might drop a coconut on him and pretend it was an accident.

Dura also keeps talking about the strangers on the island, the ones the adults speak about in hushed tones. Bumbu Joshua says we need to call on our ancestors to keep them away, and that they may destroy our island culture. I don't understand it; how can they change our people and our way of life? But I've seen them too… an unknown boat here, an unknown person there. Nothing good can come of it, they say.

I hardly even think about the end-of-year exams, while my legs are clamped around the trunk halfway up to the sky. I hold on tight to my machete, the bush knife Bumbu Joshua gave me, which I keep sharp at all times. I whack at one of the heavy pods and listen to it hit the ground; then another, and another. Leaving the smaller ones for later, I let my eyes roam over the panorama again. They come to rest on the island of Maevo, and further out, on Tutuba and Malo. *Where is the big island of Pentecost?*

This thought tears through my stomach like a lightning bolt. My hands turn sweaty and weak, and I feel the bush knife sliding from my grasp. Instinctively, my hand catches hold of the falling object.

What a fast reaction, I congratulate myself, breathing a sigh of relief. Anyone who might have walked below me might have gotten sliced in half, had I not had such presence of mind. My right hand still clasps the blade firmly when big drops of blood turn the sharpened metal and my hand crimson.

An ear-splitting scream emerges from my chest. I drop the blade. Blood spurts out of my hand, and I fold my fingers to close the cut. *Did I see bone through the open gash?*

The island starts to spin, and soon, the whole jungle is in a wild dance. My stomach cramps. I feel faint, but twenty feet is too far to fall. So I hold on, strangling the tree with my uninjured limbs. I take a deep breath and pay no attention to scrapes and splinters as my legs slide down the rough bark.

"Hold on, Abel, you can make it. You're almost down. Hold on!" Bumbu Joshua coaxes, suddenly below the tree.

Bumbu Joshua's hands pull me the last few inches, helping me drop to the ground. There I lie, heart racing, wondering if I'm going to die from losing so much blood. I try not to move a muscle. Just then, my stomach constricts as if a coconut had landed on it, and I vomit.

"Sit up, Abel," Bumbu Joshua commands. "Show me your hand." I obey but avert my eyes, swallowing hard to stop my stomach from repeating its violent heaving.

While I feebly extend my arm, I try not to look at the wound. Instead, I gaze into the canopy of the trees that surround us: coconut palms, paw-paw trees, breadfruit and mango trees swinging and swaying wildly. I can feel the spurting blood, and I feel weaker with each gush. Bumbu Joshua breaks a branch from a dondakaya bush, chews some of the leaves and adds the rest of the shoot to our harvest. Then he opens my right hand. Even though I don't want to look, my eyes steal a glimpse. The white bone that connects the thumb to the wrist shines back at me. The blood, a lighter red now, pulses out of my hand with every heartbeat. Then panic hits me like a flying arrow.

This is dreadful, awful, terrible! I need this hand for everything. How can I climb, use my knife, dress myself, even hold a pencil? That's when a more pleasant thought comes to my mind: *Surely, this will prevent me from having to leave our tribe at the end of the school year.*

Bumbu Joshua gently closes the gash and spreads the green paste across my palm. He tears off his tattered t-shirt and wraps it around my injury. Miraculously the blood stops flowing. He hugs me tightly, giving me back some of my strength and courage as his slow, steady heartbeat quietens mine. He seems as ancient as the forest around us. Even though I am already twelve, I am grateful to be wrapped in Bumbu Joshua's wisdom and care.

I had been looking forward to this trip to the mountain garden. We come here every few days to harvest coconut, taro and papaya for dinner. This Saturday was special, because I had already shot a bird with my slingshot and received lavish praise from my grandfather. The thought of pulling the rubber on a slingshot with my injured hand now makes me cringe.

"Thank you, Bumbu. You really do know everything." I stare at the green paste that sticks to his fingers.

"Ah, my boy, the forest supplies our every need. In time you will learn all about it," Bumbu Joshua's full lips curl into a smile as he stretches out his sinewy brown arm to help me back onto my feet. His bare chest is covered with little curls of white hair.

The lines on his tight belly seem like waves that refuse to be tucked into the elastic waist of his worn shorts. Bumbu Joshua proudly wears a long gnarly scar on his right upper thigh, the trophy of a pig-killing ceremony during his initiation into manhood. I may end up with a scar not unlike his, unless I lose my hand entirely.

"What if I'm never able to use my hand again?" I ask Bumbu Joshua, fearing life as I know it is over. "What will I do?" Tears cut off my voice. *I guess I can still be a teacher, even if I'm a left-handed one.* It calms me down a bit as I imagine myself, one-armed, surrounded by students.

"You will not lose your hand, my boy. And even if you did, know that you would be no less of a man. You can learn to do everything with your other limbs. But you are young yet. It will heal." I focus my attention on his sinewy arms as he ties up our harvest of various fruits and roots into two parcels. He slides a pole through these bundles for carrying the produce home. He pauses, and then he lays it across my shoulders.

"Let's go," he says, as he bends down to pick up my bush knife off the ground.

"This knife will need some work." Bumbu Joshua spits on the blade to better inspect it. Then he beckons me to lead the way home. As I walk to the rhythm of the two pendulums, I rest both hands on the pole for balance. Gradually, the pain in my right hand diminishes. Bumbu Joshua keeps a steady pace behind me with our dog, Lokin, panting alongside us.

As soon as we arrive back in the village with our harvest, my brother Dura and cousin Toa come running. They yell a greeting and check what we have brought back. When we enter the grass hut that is our kitchen, Bumbu Janet is sitting in the far corner, grating green bananas. She doesn't pay much attention to our arrival.

She's already sorted out cabbage leaves to prepare simboro for dinner. Usually, I love to help her mix the starches with coconut cream and wrap a spoonful of the mix in banana leaves. She then boils these parcels in water until they float back to the top. My mouth waters.

"What's that flapping around your hand?" Toa asks with surprise.

Bumbu Janet's eyes fasten onto the green t-shirt, and before she even opens her mouth, I know the words she is going to hurl at us.

She is small and wiry with a head of short-cropped hair. Her mouth usually flashes a lovely smile, but it can also be the source of very sharp words. "Joshua, you were supposed to take care of the boy," she hisses.

When I was only two years old, I was given to the family of my father's father, as is the custom when families get too big. I often wonder why they chose to have me live with my grandparents. Was I weaker, slower, or smaller than their other children? Did I require more attention than they could give? So far, I have not been brave enough to ask.

I consider Bumbu Joshua and Bumbu Janet my parents, and I love them more deeply than Viralongo and Lovatu, my actual father and mother.

Bumbu Janet unwraps the makeshift bandage, moistens a rag and wipes my palm with it. I wince. With each swipe through crusted blood and green leaf paste, the red rim of the cut becomes more visible. It crosses my whole palm and goes deep. She reapplies more of the green paste and wraps my hand in a new bandage.

It stings. I bite my lip. For the hundredth time, my thoughts revolve around the fact that I may never be able to use my right hand again; it's going to be useless for grabbing on to anything, especially my machete. I can't climb a tree; I can't pull up a taro root; I can't even hold a fishing rod. What good would I be to my family in this state?

For that matter, if I can't use my hand, I won't be able to complete my final exams. I can't even hold a pencil. If I fail the exams, I won't need to worry about having to leave my family and all I hold dear. The decision would be taken away from me, I realize. A smile spreads across my face. But then again, what a disappointment I would be to Bumbu Joshua and my family. My smile falters.

After Bumbu Janet is done with her surgery, I slump into a corner and hug my throbbing arm. Tears burn in my eyes as I suck in the air with a ragged breath.

"How can you let this boy use a bush knife?" Bumbu Janet scolds. She has reprimanded Bumbu Joshua often for it, and this accident, of course, is fresh ammunition.

Bumbu Joshua is undisturbed. He answers with his usual half smile, gesturing with his arms. "Abel was doing a great job picking papaya and coconuts. These things happen. Calm down. Sometimes this boy just needs to concentrate better." He and I know these comments go in one ear and out the other. They won't change her mind.

Bumbu Janet continues to tell him off with words neither Bumbu Joshua nor I ever want to hear again. He tries to resolve this quarrel as fast as possible and holds up the bird I shot this morning, interrupting her complaints.

"Look, Abel shot a nalaklak bird with his slingshot. Pretty soon he'll be able to shoot a kangwae pigeon, and you know how skittish they are. I love to watch this boy take aim and shoot. Toa will roast the fowl for dinner."

I wish I had not put Bumbu Joshua in such an adverse situation. I glare at Bumbu Janet. No one else would ever address Bumbu Joshua in this way. After all, he is the chief of the Lolotitimba tribe and the head of the Hivoliliu clan on Ambae Island in Vanuatu. *What an opposite pair she and Bumbu Joshua make.* I am sure if it were up to her, she would not let me use a knife until I have a beard.

Bumbu Joshua is sitting in his carved-out timber trunk that leans against the navele tree, resting his legs, his bush knife at his side. I am leaning against the tree, too, not daring to leave.

"Your mountain garden seems to be more important than anything here in the village," she continues to nag from inside the smoke-filled cooking hut, where she is boiling pandanus leaves for weaving. Smoke oozes through the thatch roof and billows through the door. Bumbu Janet cannot see us, nor can we see her.

"If Abel leaves the village, you know that you must give up the mountain garden to Viralongo. You're too old to go there without the boy." She pauses to catch a breath. "I will certainly not go back up there at my age, and you shouldn't either." She has to control her breathing because of the smoke, so her words are barked rather than spoken.

"Do you really think that when he comes back from boarding school, he'll still be interested in our way of life? Today's children forget their bush skills when they go to school overseas. They become lazy, sit in comfortable offices and forget about the rest of the world around them, including us."

She can't be serious. "I will always want to live this way!" I almost shout at Bumbu Janet in anger. "I love the mountain garden as much as Bumbu Joshua does. And he's my very best teacher."

It looks as though Bumbu Joshua is contemplating the words that come from the hut. He is looking at me in a curious way, maybe considering whether he should take the bush knife from me. I try to cradle the knife's shaft in my palm, but I can't open my hand. It hurts too much. I drop the machete beside me.

I think back to when Bumbu Joshua taught me how to use this knife to peel tree-bark, clear paths and cut firewood. He taught me to scale the trunk of a coconut palm and tease a green fruit from the bunch with my bush knife. He showed me how to chop it with a few whacks to get to the refreshing juice inside. Without my machete, I would often be thirsty, since our village has neither a river nor a well. The rainwater we collect in cement tanks is only suitable for washing, and for watering our animals and plants.

Bumbu Joshua made a slingshot for me when I was only five. "Hit the tree trunk, Abel," he used to say, and later, "Hit the branch." Eventually, he'd command, "Now aim at that fat wood pigeon."

It didn't take me long before I succeeded in killing such a fowl or one of the flying foxes that criss-cross high in the trees above. When I did, Bumbu Joshua would wring its neck and slit open its underside to clean out the bowels before bringing our spoils back to the village to feed our family.

"Keep practicing, my boy, to become a good hunter," he says out of the blue, bringing me back to the present. "After all, all the meat we need is either running on the ground, swimming in the sea below, or flying in the sky above. You need to outsmart the prey. This way, you never go hungry."

"And all our fruits and vegetables are either buried in the ground or growing on a tree around us," I add with a smile.

"He'll learn to be more careful," Bumbu Joshua almost shouts for Bumbu Janet's benefit. "All of us have had some accident or another. It's part of growing up."

Turning to me, he says more quietly, "You are not going to catch another machete with your bare hand, will you, my boy?" He winks at me with a smile, and I feel in my chest how much I love him.

"Of course not! I'll never do that again, ever. I don't want to leave you, Bumbu Joshua!" I declare loudly, hoping Bumbu Janet would hear me too. Yet, deep down, I know I may not have a choice in the matter.

Out of our Hivoliliu clan, this big family where I have many brothers, sisters, cousins and friends, only I was offered the opportunity to pursue higher education. When my teacher suggested the idea, Uncle Toka accepted it with honor in the name of the whole family. He is my mother's brother and in charge of my future, as uncles are. How much say does Bumbu Joshua have, and how much do I? Bumbu Joshua is looking at me thoughtfully. My whole future depends on the result of the end-of-year exam.

From afar, I hear Papa Viralongo yelling in his house, which is swarming with eight children and twelve grandchildren. I think they loathe the fact that he commands immediate and absolute obedience to his wishes. Mama Lovatu thinks I am being overprotected and spoiled by my grandparents, so I am often glad not to be part of that bunch.

==//==

The sun is about to set, and several of my brothers, sisters and cousins have joined Bumbu Joshua and me under the navele tree outside our cooking hut. The evening breeze brings welcome relief from the heat of the day. Bumbu Janet and my mother are working on dinner. One by one, other siblings and cousins arrive to share the evening meal, and everyone helps with the preparations.

"Abel almost died up in the mountain garden," Dura is the first to comment on my hand. Some of my younger siblings come over to examine the involuntary surgery. "Lucky he had Bumbu Joshua there to rescue him." He turns to me and asks conspiratorially, "Did he have to climb up the tree to get you down?" The image prompts smirks and giggles all around.

"Here, I just sharpened my machete. Do you want to catch it with your left hand?" jokes Alain. "Lokin wouldn't mind a few roasted fingers." I grimace. If my hand weren't so sore, I would sock him in the face.

Bumbu Janet and Bumbu Joshua have quieted down. Presently, they are avoiding each other. Bumbu Janet is upset. I feel bad for being the one who caused the strife, and it weighs on me while we sit around the fire after the meal.

Bumbu Joshua, in his usual carefree manner, is telling us stories of the creation of our people. He knows how certain ancestral spirits influence our actions and lives, and he also seems to know everything about everyone in our village of Vatuhangele. When he's done with his story, he asks us about school and life, our hopes and worries. This is my favorite part of the evening.

Viralongo approaches our group with long and hasty steps. "There are some men waiting for you at the nakamal," he says to Bumbu Joshua.

"Must be the business people from Tanna," Tari says, running a hand through his blond hair and looking as if he knew.

My ears perk up. "Let me go to the meeting house with you. I want to meet these foreign people," I ask. When I am near Bumbu Joshua, I feel like a flourishing ndandakwora tree swaying proudly in the breeze beside a majestic banyan tree. I love to listen in on the various conflicts that arise among the several dozen people in our village: it may be a land dispute or parents objecting to two teenagers who want to be together.

I imagine going with him to the nakamal, where men share the customary drink of kava. They say that half a coconut shell of this fermented brew calms men down. Bumbu Joshua manages to stay serene and undisturbed, even in the most challenging situations. Most of the time, he is able to restore peace by finding a solution both parties can accept.

"I heard these people have boatloads of money," Vira adds. I wonder if he's picturing that in his mind. "And they wear expensive sunglasses and golden bracelets." I can see he wants those things, too.

"We should throw them out sooner rather than later. They may be dangerous." Dura is repeating snippets of conversations he's picked up here and there. "They've come to change our culture."

"How old are they?" I wonder out loud. Are they approaching

the age of wisdom Bumbu Joshua has reached, or are they brash young men, maybe fresh out of school? My curiosity tempts me to sneak to the nakamal and hear what's going on with my own ears. In fact, I want to talk with the men and learn about their business and their intentions. I want to know what powers they have that might change our way of life.

I don't want Bumbu Joshua to leave the fireside. He has asked us important questions, and we have things to say. But he starts the process of getting up from his dugout log, grimacing and leaning heavily on my shoulder. Bumbu Joshua's knees tremble, and they refuse to straighten completely. His frame unfolds into a vague Z shape, making him scarcely taller than I am. For the first few staggering steps, he relies on the support of his cane. Then he regains his balance.

"Can I come?" I'm begging now.

"Stay with Bumbu Janet," he mumbles softly. Then he embarks on the footpath that snakes towards the nakamal. His figure is soon swallowed up by the tree ferns and shrubs as he labors up the slope to the men's clubhouse. Lokin, tail wagging, accompanies Bumbu Joshua instead of me. I'm disappointed and slouch against the navele tree with sagging shoulders.

Bumbu Janet doesn't pay me any heed as long as she knows where I am and what I'm doing. But I swear she has eyes in the back of her head. If I try to sneak out of her sight to pick ripe cocoa pods or to scale a tree, or if I decide to play with my cousin next door without telling her, she's right on my tail. When she calls my name, she expects me to answer instantly. Failing to respond in two standard calls can result in serious trouble.

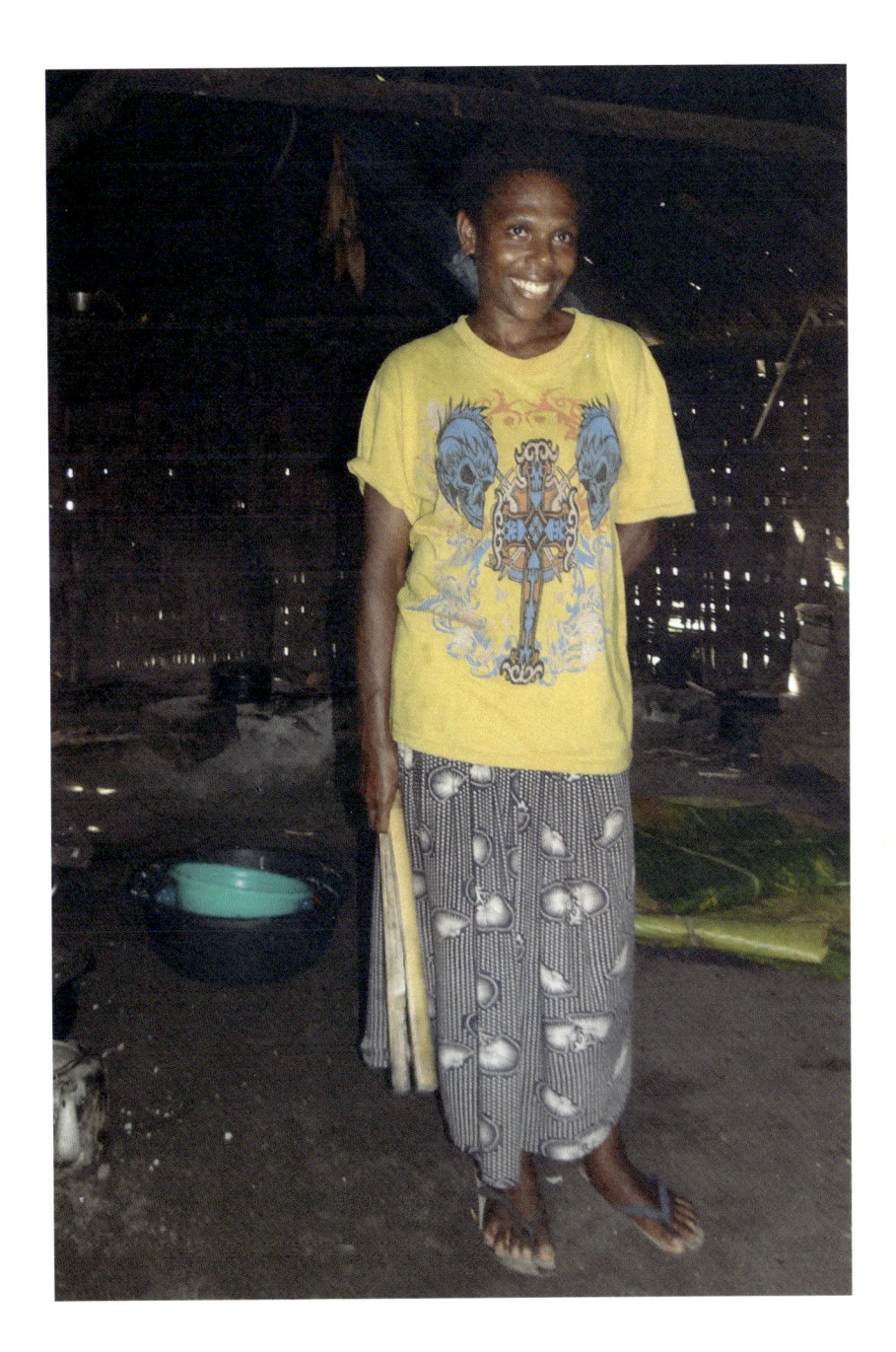

11

That's when she uses her coconut broom for "educational purposes," as she calls it, and I end up with a sound thrashing at mid-buttock range. Her left hand tightly holds me by the arm, foiling any attempt at escape. Her right hand, empowered by its woody extension, sends me jumping and yelling.

Today I am not going to take that course. Bumbu Janet asks me to feed the pigs, and I obey. Then I go and sit in my perch in the guava tree and feast on some of the sweet fruits that have ripened behind the bush hut kitchen. I don't need my bush knife to open them.

Bumbu Joshua returns after dark. Most of the fires have burnt themselves out, and the birds have quieted down. He surprises us with a plucked rooster that someone offered him at the nakamal to thank him for his advice. He ties it to the rafters inside the kitchen hut.

It is time for the boys and men to retire to the men's sleeping house and the girls to the women's. I am so tired that I could fall asleep leaning against a tree. It's been a long day, and my hand aches. I know Bumbu Joshua's knees ache, too. He says it helps when I massage them. What if I skipped it just this once? Would he say anything? He would not, I'm sure. But I'd feel bad for not doing what I can to make him walk better.

I patiently support his fragile body on the way to the sleeping house, where he drops onto his cot without a word. He must be tired, too. As my left hand finds the knots in his swollen knee, he hums a tune, tapping his fingers on the bamboo wall. Tonight it's the rhythm of a Kastom dance that the Lolotitimba tribe performs at a funeral. I prefer to imagine that parts of these melodies are Ambae love songs.

Usually, Bumbu Joshua dozes off before me, but tonight I'm worried I'll fall asleep first. Soon, though, his almost toothless mouth whistles gently as he draws in his breath, and his tapping fingers slide to his side. He's moved on to dreamland. His snuffles mingle with the sounds of cicadas and the cries of nocturnal birds for my nightly lullaby.

Even though I'm exhausted, sleep won't come, and I lie with my eyes wide open. The more I think about going away and leaving all this behind, the more it feels like a rope is tightening around my chest. I can barely breathe. How many more times will I have the opportunity to fall asleep with Bumbu Joshua? What if my right hand doesn't heal? Will I learn to hunt with my left or will I have to depend on others to feed me?

I think of old Bumbu Celeste, who's been lying in her cot for several months with heart troubles from eating a poisonous barracuda. Her relatives take turns feeding and washing her. It's not easy to while away the time when you can't do anything.

"Catching a machete with your hand… how dumb must you be?" I heard the words Tari pitched to his cousin Paul, and they hurt.

"If he loses the hand, Joshua's plans of making him his successor will come to naught," Paul responded.

Losing a hand is still better than decapitating someone who's under the tree, I justify to myself over and over. Still, it was thoughtless, maybe even dumb. *How one moment of inattention can change a whole life. Perhaps I'm not cut out to follow in Bumbu Joshua's footsteps after all.*

Chapter 2: Village Education

"When you sit at home listening to your exam results on the radio, remember that the sun will go on rising and setting, no matter what your score." The words of our teacher's farewell speech are valid, even if they are not very reassuring. One day I want to be able to say these words to a class full of my own pupils. It seems to me that being a teacher is the noblest of all professions.

In ten days, all the parents of Vanuatu will be glued to their radios to hear their children's test results. Until then, I won't know how my life will turn out: I will either stay here or go to the island of Pentecost to study things I need to survive in a city, maybe even to teach future students in our village. Either I will earn my livelihood by working the fields and fishing in the ocean, or I'll come back as a teacher. Ten more days. A nauseating chill settles in my stomach.

It is the middle of December and the end of our last year of school. We just wrote our final exams, during which my right hand hurt me so much I couldn't properly hold a pen. So I used the left to clumsily scribble an x here and there and jot a few words down where I had to. Even I struggled to decipher some of my responses. Cheeks burning, I focused on making my answers legible right up to the last seconds before we had to hand in our papers.

"I can't believe we have to wait a full ten days! I can't stand it." I lament, as my schoolmates Tari, Vira and Kwevira and I are walking along the beach for the hour's trek to get home. Here the waves lick the fine sand, and in other places, they smack against giant black volcanic rocks. We have often joked that we wished a boat would take us to school. Now my wish may come true, except that the boat will take me to a strange land.

"Hey, let's take the inland path and pick some coconuts and breadfruit to bring home. Maybe the mangoes are already ripe," Vira suggests.

"You know we are not supposed to pick those. What if the owner catches us?" I ask. Tari rolls his eyes.

Just then, the daily rainclouds roll in from the ocean. I can hardly distinguish the black cloud of dread that hangs over me from the one that darkens the jungle. Quickly, we each pick one of the gigantic, waxy leaves of the elephant plant and fold it over our heads and satchels to protect us from the squall. As we continue on our path, our talk reflects the excitement of the last six hours.

"I'm sure I aced all the math questions, except for the last one. How did you do, Vira?" Tari asks as the first big drops roll off his leaf. When it comes to mathematics, Vira is usually the first to understand a new formula our teacher proposes. He is the one with the darkest skin among us, and he has the most adventurous spirit.

"I couldn't remember the arrival date of the first European explorers," laments Vira, not even heeding Tari's question.

"In 1606 a Spanish expedition came," boasts Tari before I can say anything. He pulls out a piece of paper from his pocket and points to the date on it. Did he look at it during the test?

Tari likes to show off. He is mighty proud of his hair, which is a golden color. A soft yellow fuzz covers his chin and his arms. He is the tallest of us and a good runner, and he looks down on others as if he was superior.

"And in 1774 Captain Cook arrived," adds Kwevira, the daughter of our pastor. She is a quiet and serious girl who loves to read and study. Her beautiful dark hair is often twirled into two thick braids that her mother fastens on top of her head. She is almost as tall as I am; that is why I sometimes ask my brother Dura to pull on my legs, hoping to make them longer.

"It does seem as if it is the end of everything, doesn't it?" I say to Tari, thinking he feels the same. The completion of our tests closes a chapter of our lives, but he looks at me in astonishment. I often end up feeling like he knows something I don't, and he won't tell me.

For four years, we were rivals. Tari was the teacher's favorite, which made me sick at times, but it also made me study harder. I'd say that Bumbu Janet needed me and decline an invitation to go on a hunting trip or join a soccer game. Instead, I'd study and answer questions I imagined might be asked in a test. How I savored every time I tipped the balance and beat him in an exam.

"I can't wait to leave and see other islands!" Tari says. He's still looking down at me, but he continues, "My cousin Paul told me there are towns with hundreds of people, shops full of stuff from other countries, and movie theaters. Paul loved living in Vila, but he's come back now that his work contract has come to an end."

"I can't see the value of working just to be able to buy goods from other countries," I reply.

"That's not the point at all. Don't you see? With money, you can buy anything. Fancy shoes, sunglasses, a motorboat to catch even more fish…" his voice trails off. I can see him imagining hauling out an enormous catch and selling the surplus to get even richer.

"Life on our island is perfect. What is the point of being in a crowd of hundreds of people I don't know?" My curiosity gets the better of me, and it annoys me, but I have to ask. "What's a movie theater, anyway?"

"That's where they show how other people live, and what they have, and what they do. Paul told me it's fantastic." Tari is obviously impatient to experience this new kind of life, to make money and use it to buy things we can't get in our village. "You don't understand anything, Abel," he sneers.

I walk away towards our hut, my head spinning with questions.

===//==

"I can't go on living in suspense like this!" I declare to Bumbu Joshua a few days later. We are in our mountain garden again, picking taro and papaya for dinner. I try to keep my hand high to lessen the throbbing. "And even if I did pass all the tests, which I'm starting to doubt more and more, there is this black cloud of having to leave you over my head. I wish I could stop thinking about it, but I can't."

"You can," says Bumbu Joshua. "The future is not yours yet. Look how you're fretting and not enjoying our last days together. Be here, not in the future. Be here, and nowhere else, with nobody else, and with nothing to do but this, my boy. That's how you escape from the gloom."

"But you need me, don't you?" I start again, trying to reason with him. "Besides, I have already learned plenty."

"Sure, if you want to be a farmer or a fisherman," Bumbu Joshua says. "But one day you will step in the shoes of your ancestors and be a leader of our clan. You say you want to become a teacher, which means you need to learn what goes on in the world beyond our island."

Uncle Toka has scraped together enough money for tuition, boarding and transportation for one in the family. Many times, he had told me that I am the one with the best grades and that they're counting on me. He'd said that only someone with education could write letters to the Australian church missionaries to help them understand our island culture better. But I wonder what would happen if I failed. I shudder.

Bumbu Joshua is a firm believer in education. However, he knows very little of what we learn in the classroom. I don't want to be unfair to him, but there are some things he will never understand.

I smile, remembering the day when I tried to explain to him how to use an isosceles right-angled triangle to measure the height of a tree: "You know the two short sides are equal," I said. "Keeping a short side on the ground, you can walk away from the trunk until, when you look at the tip of the tree at a 45-degree angle, the hypotenuse exactly connects the ground with the tip of that tree. Then you can measure your distance to the trunk, and this will be the height of the tree." Bumbu Joshua looked at me as if I was speaking an alien language; as if a pig was trying to communicate with a rooster. Since then, I secretly decided not to share certain school knowledge with him.

On the other hand, he knows what plants to eat or use as medicine, how to bring about peace in a discordant situation, and how to stay happy and content. These are not things that find their way onto a school exam.

He stops in mid-pull, releases the leaves of the taro plant, straightens up laboriously, and fastens his pale eyes on me. His broad smile and his calmness make me hopeful that he knows a way out of my situation. Surely he has a solution for my woes, as he does for those who consult his wisdom in a tribal meeting. He probably has special powers. A rush of love and admiration for Bumbu Joshua washes over me. How honored I consider myself for all the attention he showers on me.

"You are fortunate to have schools, my boy. There were no schools on our island when I was young. I only learned to read and write from missionaries when I was an adult. I never had the chance to learn things like English, or math, or science. You know a lot more about these than I do. And now it's too late to learn them."

He squats down again and tightly grabs the base of the taro leaves. Pursing his lips in full concentration, he shakes it and pulls until the uprooted taro root slams onto the grassy patch near my feet. He sighs contentedly. He loves to teach me what he knows, and I am eager to listen, even if he tends to ramble. He's definitely in the mood to talk, and I want to get my mind off my worries. I can't stop myself. I think this question will be a challenge for him.

"Why then are there cyclones, Bumbu?"

"Ah, little man," he pauses to recover his breath. One last tooth remains as an outcrop on his bottom jaw. It is close to the front, quite nicely displayed. He relies on it for steering his speech. "The cyclone is for regeneration and strength. Consider the moon cycle. It brings the seasons for everything: planting, fishing, hunting, breeding; you name it. Anything that grows is tested for strength by the cyclone. Such a fierce wind requires deep and large root systems and strong branches."

Ah hell, there he goes, I think, while I refocus my attention on his hands.

"Look at the giant nakatabol tree and its enormous root system. The tree grows fast during many moons. It seems it can sense from experience that a testing time will come." He takes a deep breath while he thinks of another example. "Look at our thatched kitchen hut. We need to make it strong enough to withstand that next cyclone."

All the while we've been bundling our harvest together into two parcels that Bumbu Joshua tied to both ends of our four-foot pole. He pauses a moment before he lays the pole across my shoulders. It's up to me to carry it home. *How good it feels to be useful.* But I understand that Bumbu Joshua has bigger plans for me than continuing this lifestyle.

==//==

Finally, the dreaded day arrives, and the whole village sits around various AM radios to listen to the exam results. I've had ten days to let the doubt grow in my thoughts, and I am pretty sure now that my dream of becoming a teacher may stay just that: a dream.

"Kwevira Benadeth passed the tests with a result of 96%," the newsreader's voice crackled on the old radio. "Tari Johnston passed with a result of 98%. Abel Nako passed with a result of 97%."

My heart almost stops.

"These three promising students will be leaving the village to continue their studies on the island of Pentecost," the announcer states without a hint of emotion. And then it hits me: what about Vira? I did not hear Vira Edmon's results announced among the best.

There must be a mistake. Vira had looked forward to leaving the island and seeing the world 90 nautical miles away. He must be so disappointed. I, on the other hand, want to stay with Bumbu and my tribe. Bumbu Joshua is so old that he might not be waiting for me when I return. How can I leave him and Bumbu Janet behind after all they have done for me?

But my fate is sealed. Now it is final: I am leaving on February 7. I look into the faces of those around me. Vira is shaking his head. His eyebrows are squeezed together.

"Hemi gat hed… I've always said it, this boy has a good head," Bumbu Janet sings out in her excited way. I look across to where she is standing, retrieving clothes from the line. Do I see a tear in her eye? I can't tell if it's one of joy or sadness, but I know she will miss me. The fact that she won't have me to yell at will surely be the most painful part for her.

She drops a t-shirt into the basket and comes towards me with a big smile, arms outstretched. Then she folds me into a hug. I feel the affection in her embrace as well as her sorrow, and I know this hug is one of dignity and respect. Both she and I know that the situation cannot be changed. We will part from each other, and that is real; we will have to learn to live with it. Her hug is sending me off to start a new life.

No more waking up with the jubilant songs of the morning birds. No more boastful crows of the cockerels calling us into action. No more morning prayers with Bumbu Joshua, who's usually up by the time I crawl out of the sleeping hut. These prayers are quite lengthy, by my standards, as he reveals his inner secrets and wishes.

A dark cloud obscures the sun, and even the cicadas fall silent. I swallow hard. *No tears, no tears, no tears now. Just like Bumbu Joshua.* He is nestled into his wooden carved seat, observing Bumbu Janet approvingly. I have never seen him cry a single tear, so I am not surprised that he does not show any signs of emotion now.

I shuffle in the direction of Lokin, who wags his tail at me, unbothered by any of my worries. After all, he does not need to go far away and over the ocean into a foreign land.

No more hunting trips with Bumbu Joshua for birds or bats. No more eavesdropping on his conversations with quarreling landowners. No more harvesting trips to the mountain garden. A sigh straggles from my chest.

"I don't want to go. I don't want anything to change. I am so nervous, my stomach is doing flips," I whine. "Do I really need to know anything else?" I ask Bumbu Joshua for the tenth time.

"You must be brave," Bumbu Joshua tells me. "Remember, you're going away for a four-year adventure. It wouldn't be an adventure if you weren't nervous. There's no progress without struggle." He pauses for impact. "It's easy to walk on the well-trodden path. Make your own path, my boy."

I almost buckle under the weight of expectations that our tribe is thrusting upon my shoulders. I don't like it one bit.

Then he adds, "You have a good head. Learn everything you can, and when you come back with all your new knowledge, you'll be a good teacher and leader for our village.

"I think you are an eagle chick ready to hatch and fly, even though you feel snug in your eggshell.

"Look at the clouds, Abel. Beyond them, there is blue sky. But before we see the blue sky, there will be rain. The rain and clouds might be an expression of sadness or fear, but things always become bright afterward. Now don't get me wrong," Bumbu Joshua tilts his head slightly as if he was listening to the Great Creator. "You might not like clouds and rain. Yet without the clouds, there is no rain, and without the rain, there is no taro, no coconut, no life. And here we are, you and I, enjoying these plants all around us. It pays to look at the balance of things." Bumbu Joshua's words make sense. I nod, and a smile forms on his lips.

"I never want to leave you, Bumbu Joshua." I look into his eyes, but he looks away. "I always want to live by what you teach me." On this island, I have thrived in the care of my grandparents like a chick protected by a territorial rooster. Who will look out for me when I'm so far away?

"Abel, we are mighty proud of you." My eldest brother Molrongo nudges me in the ribs. He owns a goat and a couple of pigs that he keeps tethered to a post beside his hut. His wealth in goods and friends makes me question the wisdom of going away.

"Remember, it's been nine years since I felt like Vira does today. I had also been pining for adventure. I know what it feels like. But you know, life is good here." He looks around. "I might even get married soon," he says with a twinkle in his eyes.

Since he keeps his love affairs very secret, I can't help but wonder whether he really has a girlfriend. He doesn't seem like he is ready. *A bit like me... not at all ready for what's coming.*

"You'll be ready when the time comes," he says, reading my mind.

"How can I know that?" I question, looking off into the distance. I've never been far from our village, and always with a family member. Molrongo smiles. He must have noticed my panicked face, because he adds jokingly, "Now that my house is built, you're leaving. Unless you reckon you can't. We'd understand that, too." He looks around. "Sometimes, a path is just too hard for us to take. You might feel too young, too weak, or too scared to go away. Besides, I need you to look after my kava plants when I'm off fishing. I could pay you in chickens," he laughs out loud.

How can Tari be so confident, even eager to go away? How could I prove my readiness? I shudder, but a daring plan starts to form in my mind.

What if I visited my mother's sister, Aunty Anna, down the coast in the far South of Ambae? Last time I saw her was at her wedding to John Tariyuke. They had both brought five children into the new family after John's first wife had died from a fever, and Anna's first husband drowned in a storm at sea. What a wedding feast it was! She has often told me I am her favorite and invited me to come to visit her sometime when I am older. I must be old enough now; if I wasn't, why would they send me away?

It can't be that difficult to find this village if I stay near the water's edge and keep walking in a southerly direction. Our ancestors were good long-distance walkers who knew the island like the palm of their hands. Bumbu Joshua, too, knows all the villages on the island by heart. He has traveled on all the tracks that connect them and knows their distances from each other. I've heard him give directions to people who have stopped in our village while traversing the island to see relatives, or to search for water and food supplies.

Braving such a daring endeavor would prove to everyone that I am ready to face the big world out there like a grown-up. Bumbu Joshua will certainly admire my boldness. He will be so proud of me for visiting a valued family member.

The more I think about it, the better the idea seems. Step by step, I map out my plan. *I will show you, Tari! Not even you have achieved such a daring feat of bravery.* This will be a story everyone will talk about for many years to come.

The next day I roll my machete into a pandanus mat. I scoop the slingshot into my pocket, which is already weighed down with carefully selected pebbles. Right after lunch, I slip into my flip-flops and take off. To avoid any unnecessary questions, I look as relaxed as possible as I stroll past the huts as if one of them was my destination.

When I reach the forest unobserved, I let out a sigh of relief. Here, where our village ends, I look back. *Off into the adventure!* Fresh energy and enthusiasm put a spring in my step. Suddenly, a movement catches my eyes, and I find myself in front of Molrongo. My shoulders drop. He's with a lady I have not seen before. She's not from our tribe. I try to hide, but he has already spotted me.

"Little brother, where are you going?" he laughs, letting go of the lady's hand.

Don't look as if he caught you, I tell myself and stand upright. As if Bumbu Joshua had sent me on this errand, I mention that I'm on my way to visit Aunty Anna and Uncle John in Lolovatali.

"Are you serious? Do you know the trekking path? You sure you want to go by yourself?" He points to my bandaged hand, some concern in his voice. "That's a three-day walk."

"Of course," I say matter-of-factly and shift my weight from one foot to the other. "I'll be okay," I say and turn to leave. He shrugs and directs his attention back to his lady friend. I breathe out and walk steadfastly towards the ocean. My step is light; the sun is shining brightly. *I did it. That was not so bad.* I congratulate myself on my brilliant idea. *I will show them!*

I reach the water's edge in record time. Now to turn south and see what comes. The walk on the white beach does not last long, and soon I have to climb over what seems to be an old lava flow thick with trees and impenetrable vegetation. The sun is burning down on me, and I am so thirsty my tongue is stuck in my mouth. The pandanus mat is getting heavier and heavier. My hand aches. *I need to find food and drink soon,* I think, veering off my path in search of a coconut palm.

No such luck. I make myself go back to the beach and hope to hunt for fish. Of course, my weapons are not adapted to that, but I do catch a few prawns with my bare hands and eat them raw after smashing their heads with a rock.

Upwards and onwards, as Bumbu Joshua likes to say. I climb the dense forest again and have to use my machete to cut a path. It is slow going, and for the first time, I start to question the wisdom of my decision.

I keep on going, taking advantage of a few more hours of daylight. All the while, I keep the ocean, no matter how far, to my right. The undergrowth lightens somewhat, and I manage to make some headway. The birdsong all around me does not help my stomach feel fuller, and loneliness starts to weigh on me. As I forge onwards, I have plenty of time to think of dangers lurking in this jungle, where to stay for the night, and how to get food. *I could eat a wild pig,* I boast to myself, imagining how I'd kill one and roast it over a fire.

A breadfruit tree offers me its pod – big, round, green and spiky. I manage to dislodge it by throwing a big stone into the tree, and then it splats before me, seeds spilling out. A bundle of black bugs in its center tells me the fruit is ripe. *Good, no need to make a fire, I can eat it raw.* I lay the pandanus mat and my machete beside me on the ground and start pulling the fibrous plant apart. Each seed is wrapped in sticky yellow strings, and I am thankful for their sweet flavor. *If only I had a coconut to drink.*

The sun is about to set, and a slight evening breeze brings some welcome cooler air. My muscles ache, and now that my stomach is somewhat satisfied, I look for a place to lie down. That's when I notice tufts of coarse hair clinging to the bark on the tree before me. *An old boar probably scratched its haunches here.*

What was that? A distant snort. My hands get clammy. A low grunt makes the hairs on the nape of my neck stand to attention. I know that wild pigs fight rather than flee, and I am not in any shape to fight a wild boar. My heart hammers. My hands shake as I grab my parcel and tip-toe into a thicket. *Hide me, crown bush.* Every muscle in my body is tense, ready to act. Bats are noiselessly looking for their dinner of flies. My heart is ready to explode. I wait.

Another snort, nearer now, a movement. A female with a young one is engrossed in foraging for food. *I should kill the young one - wait, what am I thinking? But the bravery of it! My famous ancestor, Bumbu Lazarus, would have done it. Bumbu Joshua, you'd approve, wouldn't you? "Brave Abel killed a wild boar!" you could say.*

I flinch at a drawn-out, low grunt. The sow has come so near that I can almost touch her. My hands shake as I grab for the liana lying at my feet. *Be quiet, heart. Calm down, hands.* Though my fingers fumble, I manage to make a lasso. Then I bide my time. The sow scours the roots of a tree for grubs. She's in my range.

With a sudden lurch, I throw the lasso over her head and tie the vine to the base of the thicket that hides me. Grunting wildly, she thrashes, jerks, and strains, but my lasso holds. She squeals pitifully as she struggles to be with her piglet. Then my victim goes wild, snorts, digs her hooves and tries to get away. Still, the liana holds.

My nerves are raw. *What next,* I ask the darkness. Every one of the sow's moves makes me jump. It takes about an hour before she calms and begins to suckle her young. *This is my chance. Should I approach them in this vulnerable state and cut off the piglet's head with my machete?* It seems cruel, but it would provide me with food for the coming days. Thinking of my brave ancestor, Bumbu Lazarus, I unwrap my blade without making a sound.

Voices shatter my thoughts. Three men appear and make straight for the tethered animal. One of them spies the pandanus mat and comes towards the bush I'm hiding in. My heart stops. I bite my hand to stifle a scream.

The one who discovered me is big and burly. He grabs me by the arm and pulls me out of my hiding place, alerting the two others with his booming voice. His friend is about my height, and rather stout, with arms as thick as my legs. The third one is rather skinny and by far the youngest of the three. He cuts the liana, setting my quarry free. The three surround me. *Now I am their prey.*

"What are you doing here?" I think my hunter says, but I can't understand a word.

"I am Abel Nako from the Lolotitimba tribe up in Vatuhangele village," I say by way of introduction in vague Bislama. They look at each other and seem to discuss what to do with me. More unintelligible words follow and obvious questions, but none that I know how to answer.

"Hemi Tabu. Tabu mo yu brekem law." I know what this means in our language, as well as in Bislama: "Absolutely forbidden. You broke the law." But what did I do? I can only send a short request to my ancestors to protect me from these men.

The leader of the three wraps his large hand around my arm and drags me off. Pandanus mat and machete stay behind, under a bush I will never find again. Soon we arrive at a cluster of thatched huts, not unlike ours. A fire is burning, giving off uneven flickers. Men, women and children emerge, and intense discussions follow. In the dark, fingers point at me, and some

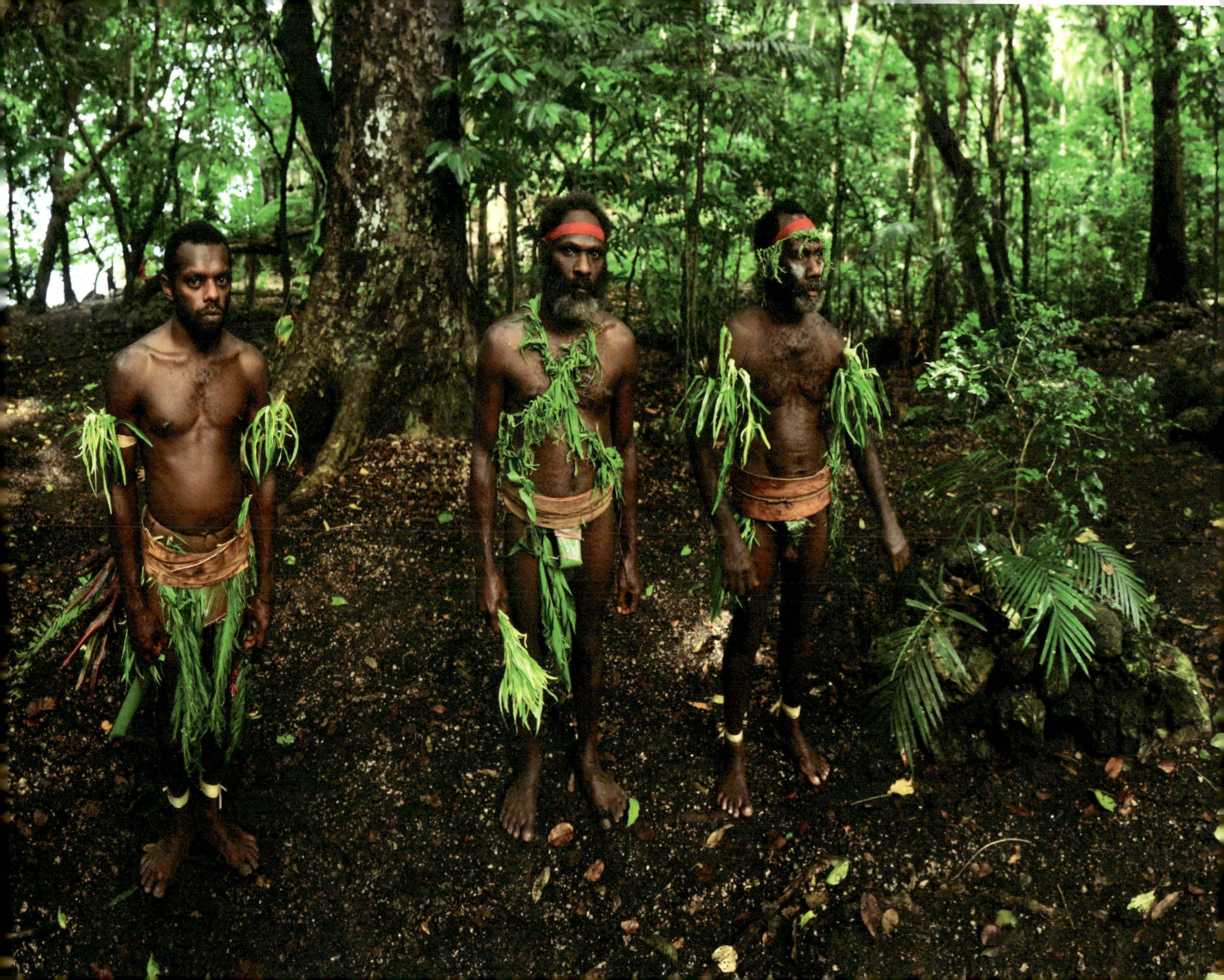

faces address me directly. I press my elbows into my sides to make my body as small as possible.

"I didn't do anything!" I shout again in our language, then in the best Bislama I can manage, and try to wriggle free. But to no avail. My chin trembles. I have run out of things to say. Either they do not understand my words or choose to ignore them.

Finally, the strong one who had yanked me into this place drags me off to the men's sleeping hut and allows me to crumble onto a cot. But he makes sure I will still be there in the morning by tying my legs to a bedpost. *What did I do to arouse such anger? What is going to happen to me?* I am confused, but more than that, I am scared. *What is the worst thing they can do to me?* One by one, the men come in and lie down. Some more words are exchanged, but gradually they are replaced by snores.

In the middle of a vivid dream of a violent pig hunt, I get a nudge in my ribs. I've slept lying on my injured hand, and it hurts. I rub my eyes with my left. Fire ants are crawling all over my cot. I jump, but my shackled leg stops me from making the move I had intended, and I fall flat on my face.

The hunter tells me with words and gestures to get up. "Lolotitimba tribe?" he asks, and I nod vigorously, happy they understood this one word from last night. After they untie me, I shake off the last of the fire ants, and we step into the morning light. Tree ferns provide shade, and flowering poinsettias nestle among giant banyan trees. But the people have not become any friendlier. Feeling the eyes of everyone upon me, I eat some bananas and drink the juice of a coconut while I scratch the burning bumps on my legs.

Sturdy's big hand around my biceps leaves me with no doubt that I am to follow where my three captors tread. His tight grip discourages any thought of escape. *Where are they taking me? What will they do to me?* I have a hard time keeping up. Half running, half stumbling, I stare ahead without seeing. My heart beats so hard I can only take little breaths. One of my flip-flops comes off.

Are they dragging me back home? Hope mingles with relief. I sigh when I realize why these unfamiliar people want to make the arduous trek to my village: They want to wrangle some restitution from our clan for whatever I've done wrong. But I'm not sure they know the way.

"Wait," I shout, but the only effect is that the grip around my arm gets tighter, dragging me on. "We need to go down to the beach," I try to tell the men, but I can't, so they don't. We hike through the woods, across ridges, into ravines, and I'm not even sure anymore if they are going to bring me back home or not. Tears rise in my throat, and I gulp down air to keep them at bay.

At last, we arrive at our village, entering by the southern entry. I still dangle from my trapper's firm grip as the men stride purposefully to the center. It's not only Tari, but also Kwevira and every other kid in our tribe who witnesses my sad return. I look like a criminal, and I can't bear it. I want to disappear into a wild boar's den and never come out again.

Bumbu Joshua gets up from his dugout tree and comes over. The men talk, gesticulating wildly, and Bumbu answers in Bislama. I understand only bits and pieces of it. A circle of nosy people is forming around our little congregation. "Tabu" I hear again and again, before the men retreat to the nakamal to discuss the matter over shells of kava. I hide in our hut with Bumbu Janet. It doesn't take long for my brothers and cousins to join us.

"Everyone was worried about you," Dura reproaches me, his arms crossed in front of his chest. "How can you take off like that? That was a super stupid idea."

Even Tari has come to rub in my failure. "Everyone knows there are wild boars in the south of the country. You can't go there without a rifle." *Ah, the wise one has spoken again.*

After what seems like hours of negotiations, the men re-emerge from the nakamal and get ready to leave. Suddenly, Bumbu Janet's mood swings from disbelief to understanding. In an abrupt outburst of anger, she looks at the assembled group of visitors and family members and asks me directly, "Did you know you had a domesticated pig in front of you?"

"No," is all I can contribute.

"There is no way of telling if a pig, or a chicken for that matter, is wild or domesticated, as it roams freely in the jungle!" Her voice rises as she formulates my defense. "It doesn't make sense to accuse our boy of stealing. These animals may have been on John Tariyuke's land, for all we know!"

The men look at each other. Bumbu Joshua, the chief mediator, looks uncomfortable at having to agree with Bumbu Janet, but he picks it up from there.

"It's true that you should have kept the pig on your land. Once it trespasses into another man's property, it is considered wild." He nods to underline what should be evident. The men are calm from the kava and stand there, listening. Before the assembled crowd of curious people, Bumbu Joshua explains again that the men thought I was stealing their pig. That's taboo!

Of course, I can see their point, as the sow was tied down and I was holding a machete. Intending to kill a mother-pig when she is still suckling a young one is another one of the taboos I violated.

Bumbu Janet, now bolder, goes on, "If you continue to hold this boy accountable for any wrong-doing, you will have to confront my brother-in-law, John Tariyuke. He will want to have a say in this matter." She goes into her kitchen hut, then comes back out holding a pandanus mat she has made.

"Use your common sense next time," Bumbu Janet says, offering the mat as a parting gift to them. Are her words directed to them or to me? "And travel safely," she adds. I'm secretly wishing that all the creeks may overflow on their way back to their village.

Bumbu Joshua offers up a goat to pay for the trouble I caused. I am struck by the different approaches these two have to balancing justice and fairness.

I also realize that if I had learned Bislama better, or if I had known the language those people speak, we could have explained the situation to each other. That way, none of this humiliation would have happened. *I must study and learn, even if that takes me away to Pentecost. Bumbu Janet and Bumbu Joshua, I'm sorry for leaving you behind after all you have done for me..*

Chapter 3: Christmas

At the ceremonial dancing ground, a group of tourists has mingled with our clan. Khaki-clad white-skinned men and women are wearing sunglasses under the rims of their hats, hiding their eyes. The village children are afraid of them. Our women and children give them a wide berth. *Foreigners in our village again. I don't like it.*

The leader of the group is a Ni-Vanuatu, dressed in shorts and a t-shirt. After a short talk with Uncle Toka, the tourists take a seat on a log. Every one of the visitors is watching our ceremony through a hand-held device.

Snake dancers celebrate their ancestry by swaying under the weight of a wooden painted serpent, held up high. Drummers pound the beat, while stomping feet surround them. This clan celebrates the gifts and talents the water snake has bestowed upon them, like speed and agility, cunning and frugality. All these gifts help the men in their daily survival.

Some tribes descend from doves and others from fish. Our clan has its origin in the octopus.

The afternoon is hot and humid. Several clans have gathered by the beach, ready for a Kastom sing-sing to celebrate Christmas. The sounds of slit gongs, guitars and drums fill the air. I think back to another grand ceremony in our village, when my eldest sister got married and had to move to her husband's clan. She was not too eager to leave our family, but Bumbu Joshua told her, "A girl is like a branch of the nettle tree – whatever ground you plant it in, it will grow." She was reassured by the wisdom in his words and looked happy during the celebrations. *Even she was more adventurous than I am.*

With arms hanging limply by my sides, my eyes wander to the bandaged hand. I feel so useless. Surely there is someone else better suited to this adventure.

Dura is painting white spots all over my body to show our clan's octopus origins. Earlier, Uncle Toka helped me make the mask I wear during the performance. The mere thought of dancing and celebrating makes me dizzy. *I can't do it*, I think and slump against Bumbu Joshua, who is sitting next to me. Little beads of sweat glisten in his curly white chest hair.

There is no way I can hold a mask over my head with my sore hand. The cut is oozing, sending throbbing pain up to my shoulder. This pain is my constant companion. Even though Bumbu Janet cleans and treats it every day, it seems to be getting worse, not better. I have not hunted anything for several weeks. Tonight, too weak to celebrate, too weak even to eat, I look at Bumbu Joshua.

"Feeling sorry for yourself?" He knows how I feel, even though I haven't said a word. I hang my head. The white spots on my belly should remind me of an octopus' cleverness, agility and strength, but I don't feel any of that right now, and I wonder where these traits are hiding.

"You can do it. Go. Dance." Bumbu Joshua reveals his one tooth in a broad smile. "Go, show up, and the rest will happen by itself."

Strength and agility, I repeat under my breath. *Strength and agility, coupled with cleverness.* I lurch forward against my will. In spite of the heat, a shiver of cold runs down my spine. Not paying any attention to my dizziness and fatigue, my feet remember their duty and begin to fall into step.

The clicks and whirrs coming from the gadgets the foreign visitors hold up are not distracting me anymore. I have stopped caring about the strange eyes watching us, about what they make of such a celebration. This is between me and the mighty octopus, the father of my ancestors. I am soon swallowed up among the other dancers. Watching my brothers and uncles as they summon the powers of the octopus fills me with energy, too. Bumbu Joshua winks at me.

Smoke rises from the hot stones deep in the earth, where the men buried the meat of a pig. Bumbu Janet is putting chicken, meat and onions on a bed of ground manioc and wrapping it in banana leaves. "Putum mit mo anian insaed," as she is fond of saying. Then she lays the lap-lap "klosap" alongside the tuluk on the hot stones. As usual, all the women are working together artfully with a lot of chit-chatting and laughter.

How I will miss my home! I look around. My family has taught me what I need to know to live here as my ancestors did. How will I forge new paths, and where will these new paths lead? *Strength and agility, coupled with cleverness: these are the talents the octopus offers to me. With those, I can do it.*

The sun is up behind the varied vegetation, occasionally shooting long rays through openings in the tree branches. The undulating smoke that rises from Bumbu Janet's kitchen dances in these shafts of light. The late afternoon is alive with birds hovering around the hibiscus and narara flowers. The roosters crow and lead the hens around the kitchen hut, expecting food scraps or coconut gratings. The pigs, tethered to the navele tree, are snorting a few yards away. Bumbu Joshua appears from the nearby bushes with an extra-large fistful of treats for them. His scent is like magic and soothes the beasts. They happily chomp away on the unexpected mouthfuls. It's Christmas, after all.

When the Kastom celebrations are over, everyone goes to the Christian church for mass. After that, young men will take their instruments and go caroling, singing Christmas songs in English and in Bislama. Today, I am too tired to join them. A deep yawn disturbs the trance I'm in on my way to the sleeping house. Only one thought fills my whole being: I need rest.

Our village is eerily quiet. As a breeze rustles in the leaves and the birds are settling down for the night, I feel utterly alone. *In a few more steps, I'll reach the sleeping hut.*

A root catches my foot at this moment and sends me sprawling on the ground. Without thinking, I raise both arms to save my face. I hit the ground with my right hand first. The bandage gets scraped off, and the cut is exposed and freshly bleeding. Pain shoots up my arm, forcing tears into my eyes.

With nobody around, and my body heavy as a log, I drag myself inside the hut and collapse on the cot. I take the old bandage and loosely wrap it around my hand.

Soon, the call of a passerine wakes me from a strange dream. Murmurs and snores tell me that the sleeping house is full. I can't stop my teeth from chattering. *Quiet, I will wake everybody up.* I try to sit up and take off the t-shirt that is sticking to me like a wet rag. But when I accidentally lean on my right hand, I yelp.

Feet approach. Bumbu Joshua puts a hand on my forehead. Several other men now assemble around my bed and murmur things I can't make out for the droning in my ears. Bumbu Joshua takes my right hand and starts to unwrap the bandage that had been cutting into my hand. I feel the blood rushing up my aching arm, but have no energy to either say anything or even to sit up.

The throbbing in my hand and arm worries me. Something is not right, but my mind is too fuzzy to think. Dizziness spins my cot, the men around it, the roof above my head. I don't remember ever feeling so exhausted.

"So thirsty," I want to say, but my mouth is too dry. No words come out. Only a whine escapes my throat. Lokin sniffs at my feet. His nose is so cold it sends shivers all the way up to my head.

Bumbu Joshua asks some men to carry me out under the navele tree. Bumbu Janet lays a cold, wet rag on my forehead. Then she drips coconut juice into my parched mouth. Never has anything tasted so good. I want to get up, but my right arm feels like it weighs a ton.

"Your fever is too high, Abel, stay where you are." Uncle Toka has joined the crowd around me. The first light of the morning reveals that my right hand and forearm are twice the size of my left. He looks worried. "He's burning up. Boys, get some garlic from the yard. Janet, boil it with ginseng and feed it to Abel. His temperature must come down."

"There's no way he can go with us on the cargo ship." Squinting into the canopy of the trees above me, I see Tari. The sunlight hurts my eyes. These words would have sounded good a couple of months ago, but not now. *I want to learn languages. I am going on that cargo ship no matter what.* But my lips don't seem to be functioning; they are not passing on my thoughts.

Unable to understand the meaning of the words whispered around me, I thrash about my cot. My limbs tremble; I can't make them do what I want. Where is Bumbu Joshua? Where are my brothers? What is everyone doing around me? *Help me*, I shout. A voice that is not mine scratches my throat. I catch a deeper breath to cry again. It hurts. Anger is boiling up in me because nobody seems to hear me. Then I drift into blackness.

When I open my eyes again, the sun illumines the leaves all around me. Bumbu Joshua is beside me, calling out to the other men.

"He's back," he shouts, and joy shines in his face. "Abel, you worried us! Uncle Toka went to the church of the Jehovah's Witnesses and brought back some western medicine. You've been asleep for two days and two nights, but here you are, back with us. That stuff works like magic."

The position of the sun tells me it is early morning. With a cough, I try to remove the dust from my throat, setting off explosions through my head. *Please keep your voices down*, I want to tell the crowd around me, but they look so happy that I don't want to seem ungrateful. It's hard to keep my eyes open for the blazing sun that sends her rays through the foliage.

I've lost 48 hours? I am suddenly aware that the days are speeding by like pigs running from a fire, bringing my departure ever closer. More than ever, I want to savor every moment I have with my brothers and friends. I yearn to join the sweaty group of boys of different ages who are chasing a soccer ball made from tied-together rags.

I try to get up, but the trees begin to dance, forcing me to sit back down.

"You rest now, and keep taking this medicine for a few more days." Bumbu Joshua puts a hand on my shoulder. "Bring the boy some rice," he commands, looking up.

Chapter 4: Initiation Ceremony

A tap on my left shoulder makes me turn. Vira's face is flushed. "Time to go," he says. Since I am the descendant of a clan leader, I must have an initiation ceremony before I leave the island, and the time has come.

Bumbu Joshua waited as long as possible for my hand to heal before announcing the date of this important rite. After all, I was supposed to kill two kangwae pigeons and a fruit bat to contribute to the feast. But no matter how much I tried to withstand the pain, my right hand did not allow me to do so. Bumbu Joshua decided to go ahead with the ceremony, saying we couldn't wait any longer. And with that, invitations went out to our relatives all around the island.

"It's not legitimate," Tari throws these sharp words into the group. "He didn't shoot the birds, so he's not fit to be an adult. And he almost started a war." His words sting because there is some truth to them.

"I did not, and you know it. It was a misunderstanding." Anger wells up as I start to defend myself, but Bumbu Joshua calms my doubts.

"Abel is a great student, he's twelve, and he's going away," Bumbu says to everyone assembled, closing the discussion.

The thought of going away still shoots arrows into my stomach. Part of me would prefer to stay behind with my other friends from school, continuing life as before. But the other part of me is ready for the challenge of learning what I can for the next few years. Today, I see my path clearly before me.

The air, filled with smoke rising from kitchens all around, is heavy with the smell and sounds of feasting. Such an honor arouses a heady feeling, and I can't stop my chest from puffing out as my eyes go from face to face. Tari is not returning my grin. I savor the fact that this time, I am part of something he is not. The wind picks up a leaf and makes it spiral upward. Maybe, just maybe, I can achieve what Bumbu Joshua and my family are expecting of me.

Uncle Ruben and Aunt Ruth of the Lovutikerekere tribe appear from the eastern trek. They hiked for three days to share this event with us – the same amount of time that I failed to spend alone when I tried to visit auntie Anna. I look away, hoping he hasn't heard about my failure.

"Here you are, Abel," he greets me. "News travels fast, my boy. That was a courageous thing to undertake by yourself, if a bit rash. I'm glad you learned from it." I blush. He didn't call it stupid, as Tari did, but it still stings. I bite my lip and help Aunt Ruth deliver the parcel of lap-lap she's been carrying on her head. She smiles and sits down with the ladies.

Uncle Ruben approaches everyone around him with a respectful handshake. Some of the ladies crack jokes about the two newcomers, as they are by far the eldest visitors. Having lived on their own on the other side of the mountains, they are also close to illiterate. I believe the "Victoria Bitter" logo on Uncle Ruben's orange t-shirt means nothing more to him than a nicely colored decoration.

The village meeting place is fuller than I have ever seen it. Familiar and unknown relatives, children, teenagers, older women and men all scatter about. Excitement fills the air. Some shout greetings and joyful exclamations; others are eagerly catching up on recent events. The uneasiness with new relatives is softening. Teenagers start to form little groups as they mingle and giggle. Laughter, shouts and chit-chat fill the air. There is also the sound of the occasional dog fight as Lokin is busy defending his territory.

I follow Vira without uttering a word. He is silent, too, as he leads the way to the entrance of the nakamal. The nasara, our ceremonial dancing ground, is freshly swept and empty. I have never experienced its significance as fully as I do now. My life is taking a momentous turn.

Near the entrance of the nakamal, Molrongo is supervising a few young boys who are preparing the kava. Earlier, he had selected a plant from the noble Melomelo family, a variety of the pepper plant, from the patch behind his house. He uprooted it carefully, so as not to break any of its tubers. He removed some of the upper branches and put them aside for replanting. The boys cleaned the roots with coconut fibers. Then Molrongo cut the roots into pieces and arranged them in wide wooden bowls, ready for grinding.

The boys are standing in a circle, each armed with a grinding stone cut from a coral reef. Holding the root with one hand, they cut the kava flesh with a rotating motion of the sharp front edge.

"Add a bit more water to the mix, guys," Molrongo interrupts the boys' chatter. "Hey, let the heaps of kava fibers fall onto banana leaves, not on the ground, Aaron."

"Look at this," Aaron now holds a handful of the mix and squeezes it. Muddy liquid oozes out between his fingers. "Eurk…" he says, and others repeat the action to the glee of all around. "Looks like Lokin has the runs." Laughter erupts all around. *I used to be one of the boys. But not today, and never again.*

Spirits are the official custodians of all meeting houses. I bow deeply as I enter our nakamal. When my eyes get used to the dark, I see Bumbu Joshua seated far back, cross-legged, perched on a log. He's trying to coax some smoke from his pipe. A circle of gray-haired elders, some squatting and some standing, make the nakamal look so very dignified. There are no women or children present. But, strangely, Tari's relatives are here.

Molrongo has entered the circle with the kava. I stare at him. He towers over a large coconut shell which is propped up on three volcanic pebbles. His hands move quickly, using a coconut sieve to strain the liquid, separating it from the root fibers. Little bubbles rise and burst as the dregs settle.

I had heard murmurings earlier that Chief Mui, Tari's uncle, would stir up trouble today. Aunt Ruth talked about it with other female relatives, but Bumbu Joshua played it down in his usual way. Bumbu Janet, too, paid no attention to the gossip because in such situations she relies on the wisdom of Bumbu Joshua. He is absolutely calm.

I, on the other hand, am worried. *That's why Tari got up before the sun rose and shot four birds to present for the feasting. And I? None.*

Chief Mui unfolds his frame from the log he's been sitting

on. He strides from the eastern corner of the nakamal assembly to the center. His snow-white beard matches his hair color, and he is tall and upright.

Chief Mui demands attention without uttering a word. He is a Vora Hangwe, a chosen one from the creator, just like Bumbu Joshua. They are both unique, talented and irreplaceable. He lets his eyes roam around the entire assembly. I hold my breath, hearing only the sound of my heart and the buzz of a fly looking for a way out.

As a great orator with a sharp wit, Chief Mui has influenced many community resolutions. Forceful and convincing, he usually gets his way, like he did when he instituted fines on villagers for breaking village rules. He is also very knowledgeable about Kastom laws and the history of our tribe.

With a deep frown furrowing his forehead, he lets his voice ring out. "As you all know, Tari descends from the great Chief Tafala of the Longwandu tribe. It is also common knowledge that the Longwandu tribe, although not direct residents of this land, were and still are direct descendants of Chief Tafala, just like the Hivoliliu. They, too, belong to the main family vine in the family tree. Therefore, according to Kastom Law, Tari has as much right to be initiated before his departure as Abel does. We've been trying to hold a tok-tok about this matter, but you never arranged it, so we bring the issue up now."

The silence in the nakamal is absolute.

"And if I may also add that the very land on which we gather today, including the ceremonial ground, does not strictly belong to this family." Without specifying whose land we are on, he lets everyone draw their own conclusions. "The contemptuous way you disregard Tari in this ceremony is unforgivable," Chief Mui continues. "You elders of this nasara, take this as a serious warning for things to come should there be no redress."

These last words pierce my whole being. *This is why Tari has been so mean to me.*

But Uncle Toka stands up instantly. With thunder in his voice, he commands Chief Mui's attention. "We thank Chief Mui for his colorful speech and the history and purported family lines therein. Unfortunately, this is not the right forum for such a discussion. Please take your seat."

I stand, uncomfortably, among the words flying through the nakamal. The whole assembly of elders is on alert as the two prominent figures make their respective points: Chief Mui's opinion is firmly planted on ancient land disputes. And Uncle Toka is protecting me, his nephew, like a hornet defending its nest.

"I challenge Chief Mui once and for all to call a Village Court in the coming days to look into his convoluted and fabricated version of history."

Chief Mui seems to evaluate the hostile emotions all around him and returns to his seat on the coconut log where he was perched earlier. He sits stiffly upright, his arms folded on his chest, ready to defend his nephew when possible.

Uncle Toka continues, "Let us not be disturbed by such tyrannical views as those expressed by Chief Mui and proceed with the ceremony."

Chief Mui is not one to let such criticism stand. He rises abruptly and cuts Uncle Toka off. Pointing at Bumbu Joshua, he threatens, "The truth will reveal itself to you two. I will turn history on its head when we meet next."

I stand there, feeling neglected and invisible, while these important matters are being aired. But I put myself in Tari's place and wonder if there is any way we could overcome this rift that has been handed down to us from our elders.

"Chief Mui, we thank you for making your point today. Let us resolve our difficulties in another meeting. Toka, please come forth and shake hands and let this interruption draw to a close," Bumbu Adam says. The two men step forth. At this point, another round of kava is served and all agree to take up the matter at another time.

Bumbu Adam declares peace, and a sense of serenity flows through the entire nakamal. The anxiety that had been building up in me, ebbs. Relief mingles with regret and understanding in a jumble of emotions.

Pronouncing the interruption closed, Uncle Ruben looks at Uncle Toka and staunchly continues, "If you would care to rise and accompany the young man." Uncle Toka gets up, lowers his head and proceeds in this fashion towards the front entrance. He grabs my bandaged hand by the wrist and ushers me to the center. His hand is moist and shaking ever so slightly.

Uncle Ruben looks around as if commanding the trees to stand still. He raises his voice and says, "A baby must crawl, a boy must mature and become a man. A man must marry and have children, and then he must become a grandfather to claim a generation." He pauses to catch his breath, takes a few steps forward, and gazes up again before he continues. The silence in the nakamal is interrupted only by an occasional cough here and there. Outside, a rainbow lorikeet screeches. I stand motionless.

"Heroes breed heroes like a mushroom-bed nurtures mushrooms." Uncle Ruben pauses. "Not everyone can become a leader. A boy must be brought up and instructed in his rightful place. Leaders may eventually become chiefs. All of you know that chiefs share their wealth or, as the saying goes, share a bite. They never eat an entire meal on their own." He stops again, no doubt thinking of such an occasion.

"Those who aspire to that post used to have to kill a pig for each social rank they climbed. The young men of our generation accomplish this by acquiring an education. But then as now, most significantly, a chief defends his people and does what is best for the tribe."

I try to comprehend the meaning of his words, but I am overwhelmed and agitated.

Uncle Ruben turns around and looks into Uncle Toka's face. "Are you ready to take this namele leaf and share the shell of kava with your young charge?"

Uncle Ruben looks at me with piercing eyes and pronounces, "You have been declared ngwalangelo, not a boy anymore, but a young man. Your leadership journey begins here. The Hivoliliu clan is proud of you. Take great care in your life journey. Respect the advice of your elders, and always, always try to find what unifies you with others, rather than what separates you."

Uncle Toka tucks the namele palm leaf into my waistband and straps it on with a bush vine. Some men hit the tam-tams in a rhythm that echoes the rhythm of my heart. I stare straight down as Uncle Toka lifts the bowl of kava with both hands.

He offers it to me by holding it close to my chest. The knot in my stomach tightens. My insides silently scream out in protest at the evil-looking juice that seems to have the consistency of mud. With my eyes half-closed, I lift the shell with both hands. The strong peppery scent fills my nose even before my lips make contact with the bowl. A small amount of liquid flows down my throat, leaving an earthy taste. The namele leaf is poking me and itching my midsection. Time is held in suspense. I gulp.

Uncle Toka whispers to me, "Take one or two small sips, and I will finish the rest." Relief spreads through me as he reaches for the bowl. He takes one step aside. I watch his Adam's apple rise twice, and then he lowers the empty bowl with both hands.

"Harikiana mana memaru maloku mai nduvingu!" he exclaims, thanking the spirits and everyone present for their attendance. One of the elders brings forward a young coconut filled with juice, for a mouth rinse. "Take a sip, gurgle and spit."

My mouth and lips have become thick and numb, and the drink's pungent taste is overwhelming my tongue. As best I can, I rinse, and I spit, while drool runs down my chin. *Not very grown-up!* All eyes in the silent assembly drill fiery holes into me. I dare not look around. I am relieved that the kava initiation ceremony is over, and I never need to drink this vile substance again.

The bubble of silence bursts into vigorous clapping, boastful shouts, and statements about my nature and character.

"Our young people are the future of the tribe," Uncle Toka says, not without pride.

"Nothing stands in the way for him to become a pilot," another elder adds, perhaps giving voice to a dream of his own.

"Or a lawyer," Uncle Ruben quips. "Anything that reaps big bucks! He might even go into politics! We've never had anybody in such an elevated position."

"Any white man's job is within his reach," Bumbu Joshua pronounces, "but we all hope Abel comes back for the benefit of the clan."

My head buzzes with all these possibilities.

The shouts explode into laughter all around. Bumbu Adam bursts out, loud enough for everyone to hear, "Maybe the two boys we're sending away will return with young women from Pentecost. I've heard about Tiaraga girls," he winks at me. "They wear tight skirts and like to show love to the boys."

What a joker, what a teaser! Even though my mind is still fixated on the numbness in my mouth, I turn red from embarrassment. This is not the first time he's teased me about girls. Although Bumbu Joshua has asked him to moderate his jokes in consideration of my feelings, the two now join in laughter until they rub tears from their eyes.

Cousin Vira comes running towards our little congregation. "Uncle Toka, the women are ready with the food preparations. Please lead everyone down!"

We step out into the sunlight.

"Stop right here, Abel," Uncle Toka says in a calm and respectful voice. His fingers quickly undo the vine and pick the palm leaves from my belly. He fastens them to the thatch roof to ward off evil spirits. Then he gazes across the assembly until his eyes rest on Molrongo. "Keep the boys busy preparing kava."

As the group makes its way down the slope, Uncle Toka ushers me to take the lead. It is early afternoon, and the sky is overcast. There is a breeze blowing from the hills to the east, gently cooling the air. This wind brings deep emotions of approval and acceptance. I bask in it fully. I want to be able to remember it when I feel lost or alone in the foreigners' land.

The women and children are waiting for us. Soon more than 100 people have settled under various trees surrounding the ceremonial ground. They are waiting for speeches, food and camaraderie. I stand tall and look around, never wanting to forget this moment.

Under the temporary shelter of coconut fronds, smells of ginger and fresh turmeric fill the air. Pots of rice, cauldrons of stewed goat meat and the rising steam from the haka baking oven confirm to everyone that the celebrations can begin. I close my eyes and draw a deep breath.

Uncle Toka stands up and demands attention from everyone. He invites Uncle Moses Vatuvui to take center stage.

Leaning heavily on a walking stick, Uncle Moses fills his lungs and bellows, "Bumbu Lazarus Hivoliliu, the High Chief, was your great-great-grandfather." He fixes his eyes on me. "He made history. He killed more pigs and achieved a higher rank than anyone who came before." All eyes are on him. He's telling the story not just for me, but for everyone in the assembled audience.

Uncle Moses pauses and takes two steps forward. Holes under his back pockets suggest the sturdy khaki pants he's wearing are his only pair. Due to the heat and humidity, he has draped his green t-shirt over his left shoulder. His naked belly slightly pops over the rim of his pants and dances to the rhythm of his words. "He will forever be known for creating everlasting peace with the other high-ranking chiefs of West, North, South and East Ambae amidst the tribal wars of those times. Lazarus Hivoliliu was so powerful that Mount Ngwala and Mount Vui-Nako shuddered when he died."

Uncle Moses catches his breath. "When this important life had come to an end, its spirit returned to lake Manaro." He takes a few steps back and throws the t-shirt on his other shoulder. Uncle Moses lets his gaze sweep over the crowd, then he raises his walking stick and points it at me. "And people like this young man will make great leaders in today's generation."

The hairs on the back of my neck stand up. I feel exposed and scoot back on the mat, wishing for it to swallow me. I don't know if I'll ever be a leader, and having everyone's eyes on me is making me nervous.

"Bumbu Lazarus lived at a time when we had practically no contact with the outside world," he continues. "There was a period when people were blackbirded, or more clearly said, stolen from our islands to work as slaves in other countries. Today, however, many of our people want to go into the world to make money or to study." Uncle Moses makes a full turn, looking at every person in the crowd. Finally, he fastens his gaze on me again. "Let me remind you that through education, leaders are created. Soon you will venture into the white man's world. But never forget that much of what you learn from the white man is foreign to us."

Nodding heads and a wave of murmurs speak approval in the silence. Without any more words, Uncle Moses turns away and heads back to his seat at the highest point on the root outcrop under the mango tree. I imagine myself walking in the footsteps of my famous ancestor, though I begin to wonder if I could do this with a foreign education.

Uncle Toka steps up again and nominates Kwevira's father, Pastor Vocor Benadeth, to say grace. Our pastor was leaning against the bamboo wall of one of the huts, listening to the speech. Now he stands up, takes off his cap and closes his eyes. He commands everyone to bow their heads.

A short prayer of grace over food swells into a prayer of thanksgiving. Pleas for forgiveness and protection are spliced with Bible quotes for emphasis. After that, there's a long speech about the obedience and leadership of Jesus. It ends with a special request for Bumbu Joshua's and Bumbu Janet's lives to be prolonged in good health. The mesmerized crowd answers with a long-drawn "Amen." Pastor Benadeth replaces the cap on his head, adjusts it, and then retires back to his original spot.

Now the feasting can begin. Bumbu Joshua is sitting on his hollowed-out log again, puffing on his grungy pipe and watching the noisy chaos. He looks proudly at me, nodding here and there in response to congratulations from relatives.

Kwevira is standing nearby at the buffet table with the women, filling empty banana leaves with delicacies right out of a frypan. I wish I could join her, but men do not concern themselves with the preparation of food at gatherings such as this. Dogs are sniffing around for food scraps and bones. They can't resist the smell of Bumbu Janet's wild ginger goat curry.

The Torotua String Band Boys, six musicians equipped with ukuleles, guitars and a tambourine, are setting up to perform. Their bass is made out of an oil drum with a string attached to a pole. The first song is "Sweet Lily Rose," a love song and a crowd favorite. Ladies wearing colorful Mother Hubbard dresses sway their hips, and some begin to dance.

Laughter erupts all around as Uncle Ruben joins in with a few unusual steps and gestures. The rhythm of the music pulls in more dancers. Now even Bumbu Janet is swaying her hips to the well-known tunes. By the time the band plays "Vanuatu mi laekem yu," everyone is on their feet.

The huge mango tree spreads its welcome shadow over all our doings. Hot and exhausted, I lay my mat on the ground and sit, cross-legged, under its branches. Several cousins and friends come to join me, while Tari is entertaining them with a joke he'd heard from his cousin Paul. Laughing, chewing and chatting, we all enjoy the last morsels of food. Tari's fingers are busy unwrapping a parcel of lap-lap. I feel watched and criticized as I clumsily use my left hand to do the same.

Does he reckon he'd be a better fit for this role? That would explain many of his snide remarks. True, Tari is taller and stronger than I am. And he is more confident. But he is not from a line of leaders of our clan, so this question is moot. Knowing we're leaving together, I wish we could just be friends. He obviously doesn't. My cheeks burn.

I push away my lap-lap. Suddenly, the way Tari is observing me makes me mad. It sets my heart racing. I get up, and almost by accident, my flip-flops kick some sand onto his plate. Mouth clenched, I join Bumbu Joshua under the navele tree.

When the party comes to an end, I accompany the men who gather at the nakamal for another shell of kava. I decline the invitation to drink with them, but I bask in the company of my elders.

The women, as always at such occasions, move quickly to wrap up extra food for the visitors to take, especially for those who have come a great distance. Bumbu Janet makes sure that no one misses out, as would be expected in those circumstances. She rolls up unique gifts of red woven mats for distant relatives. These mats and their meaningful patterns keep the family ties sound and strong, like the vigorous root system of the great banyan tree.

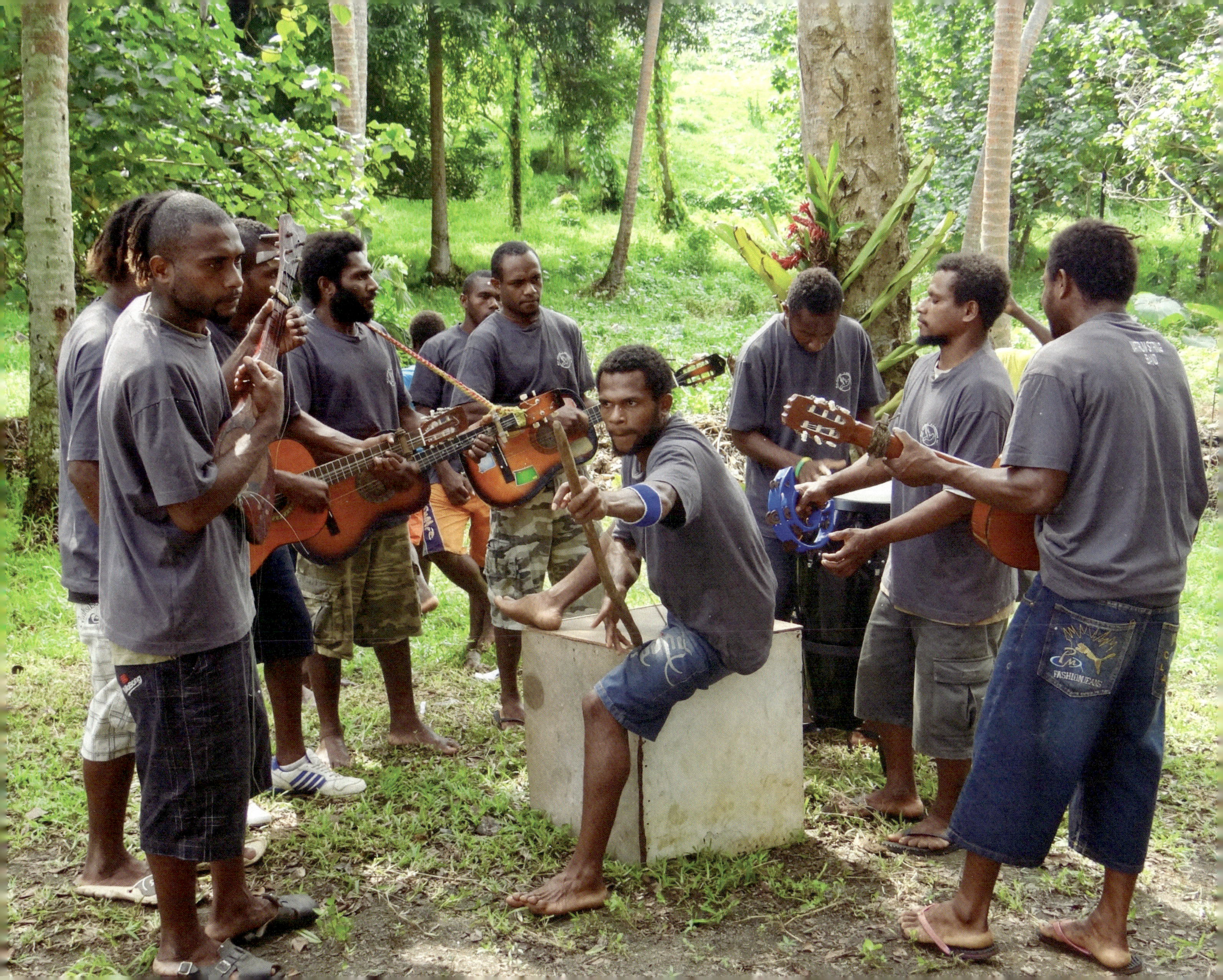

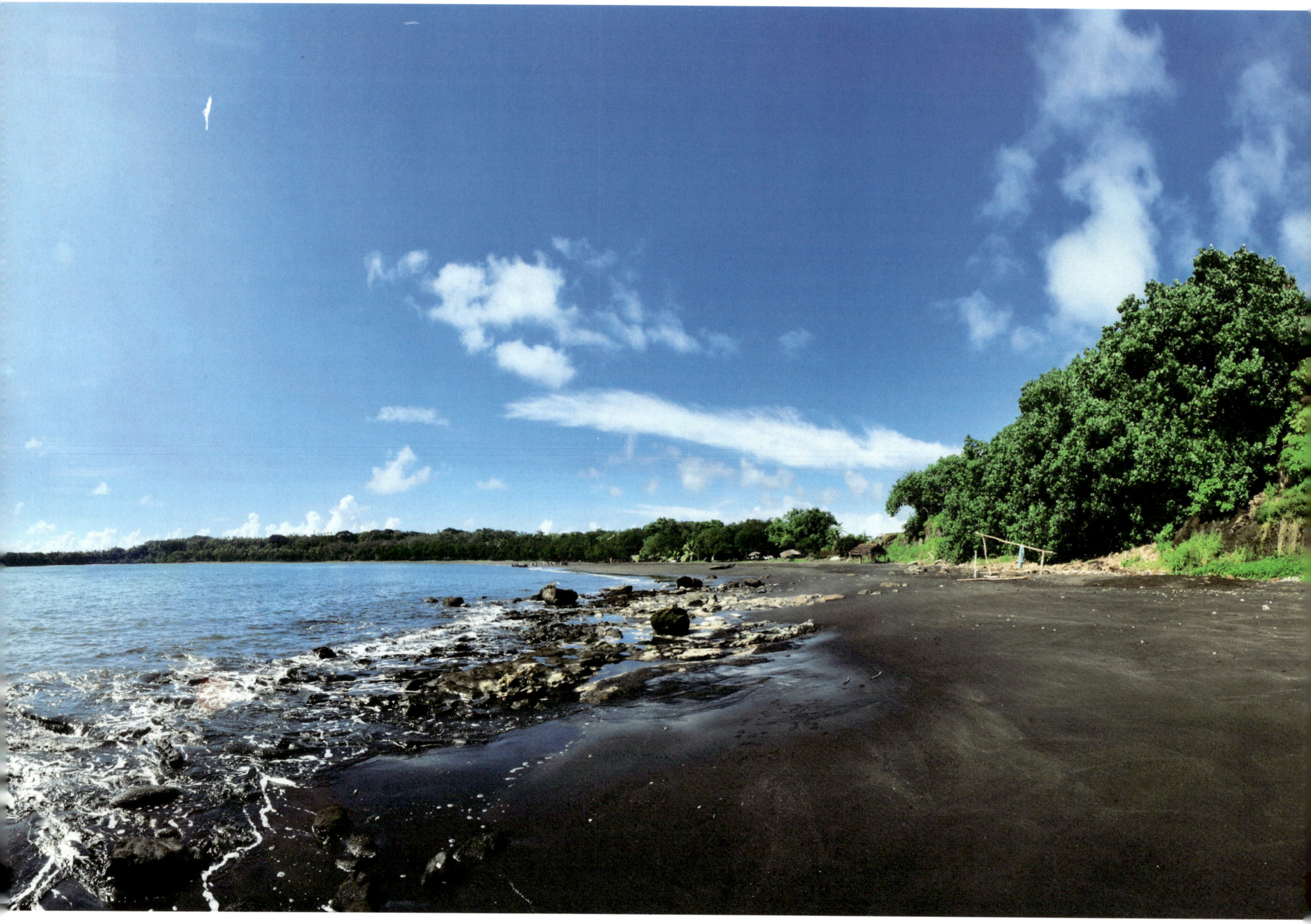

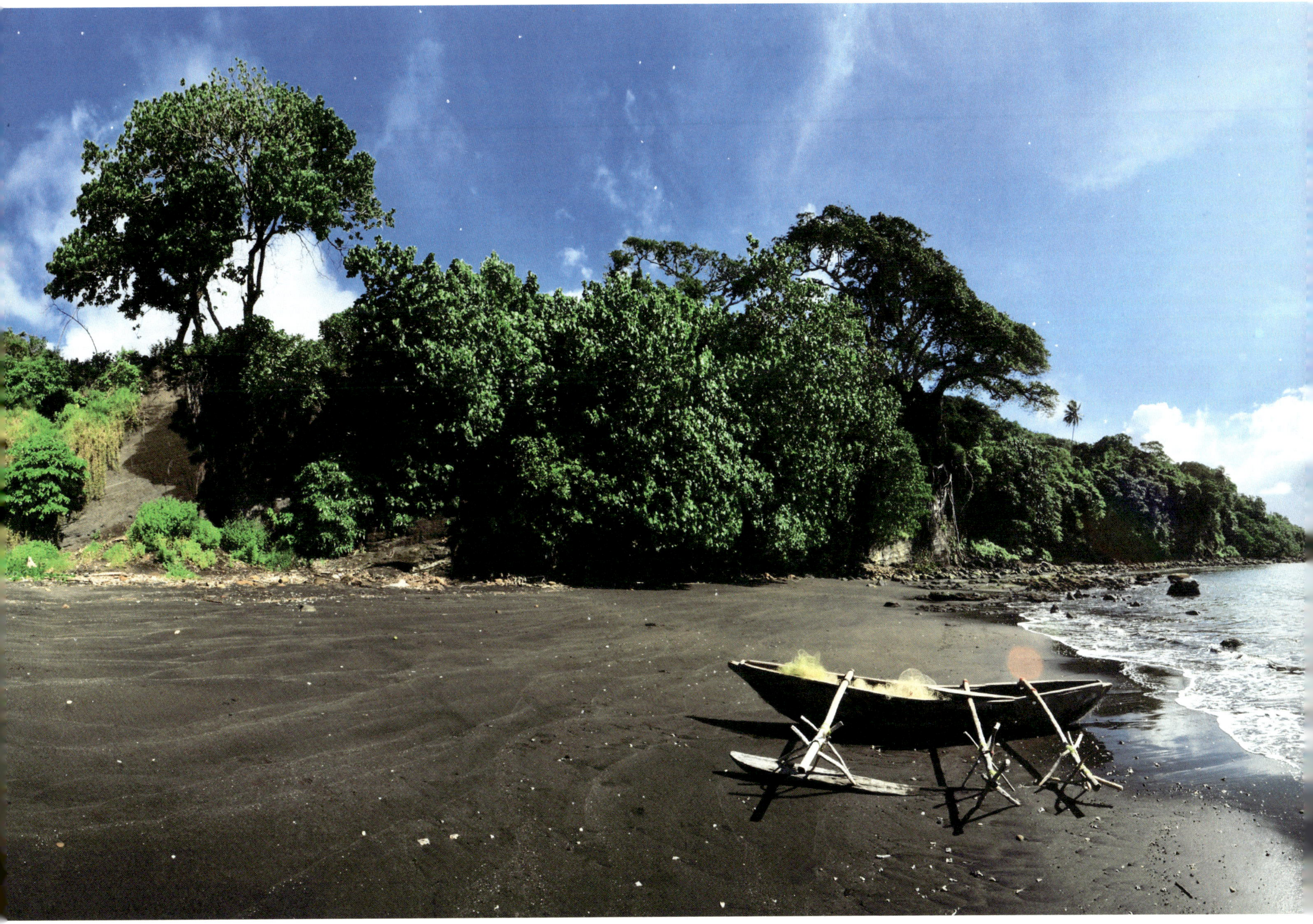

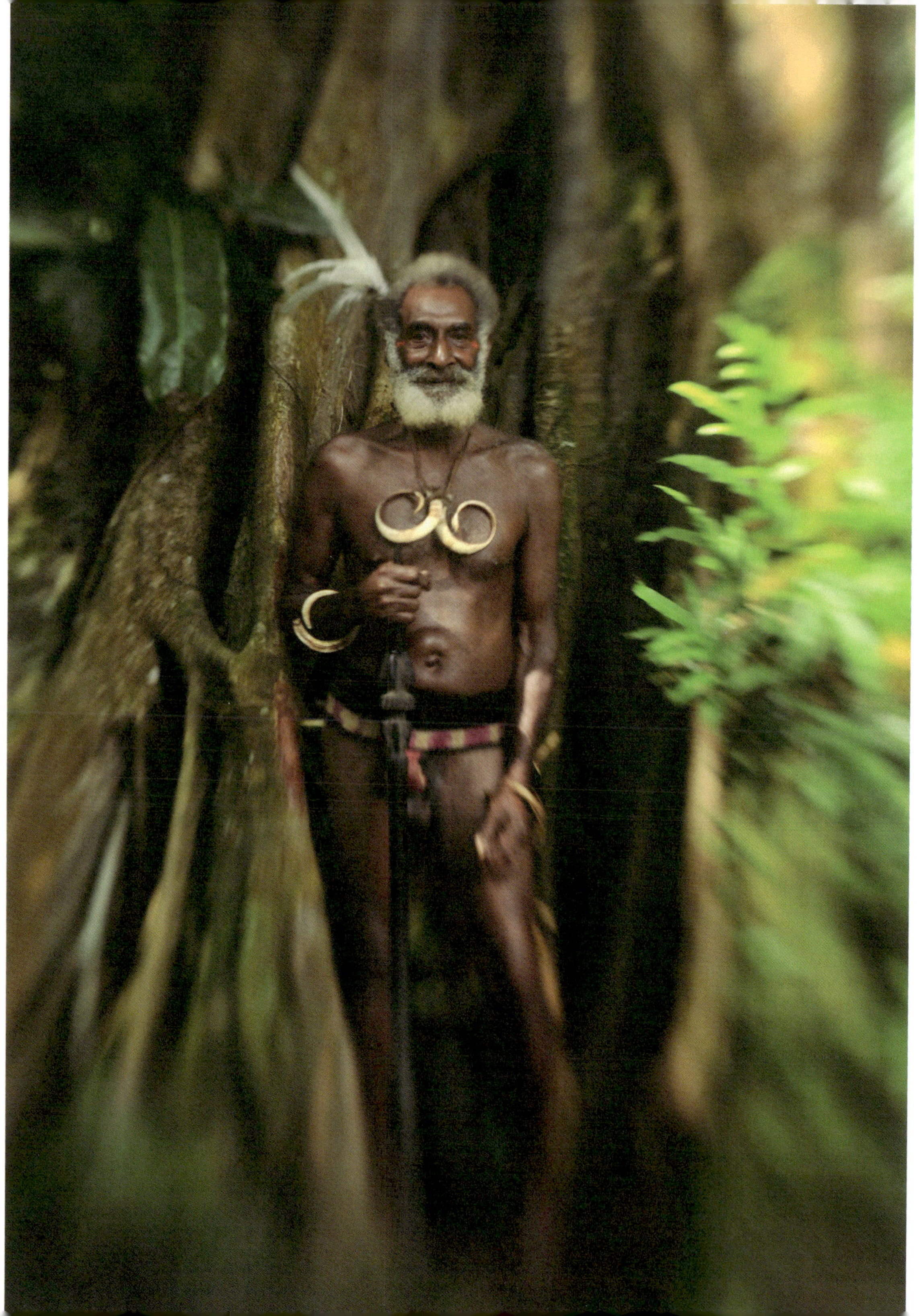

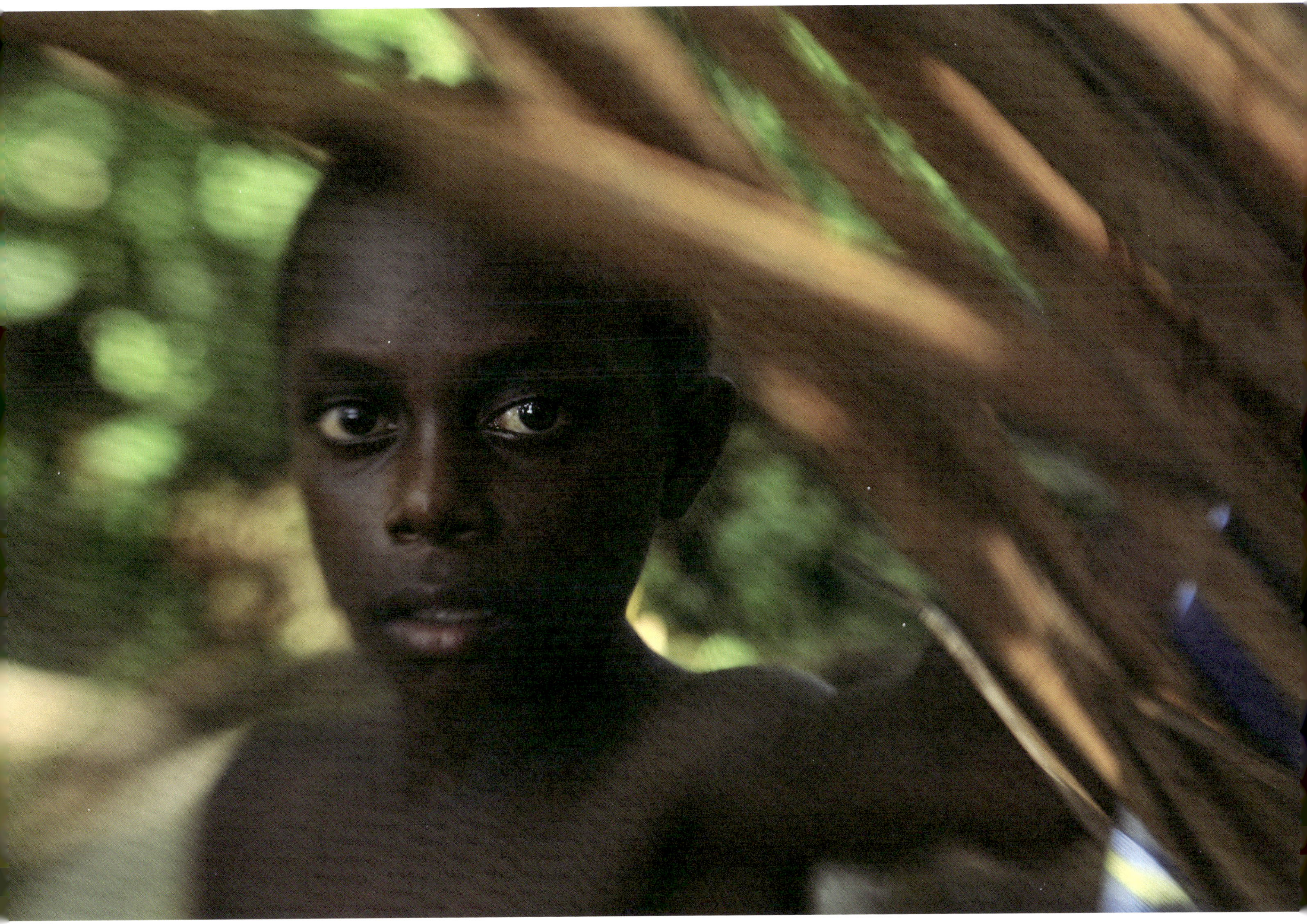

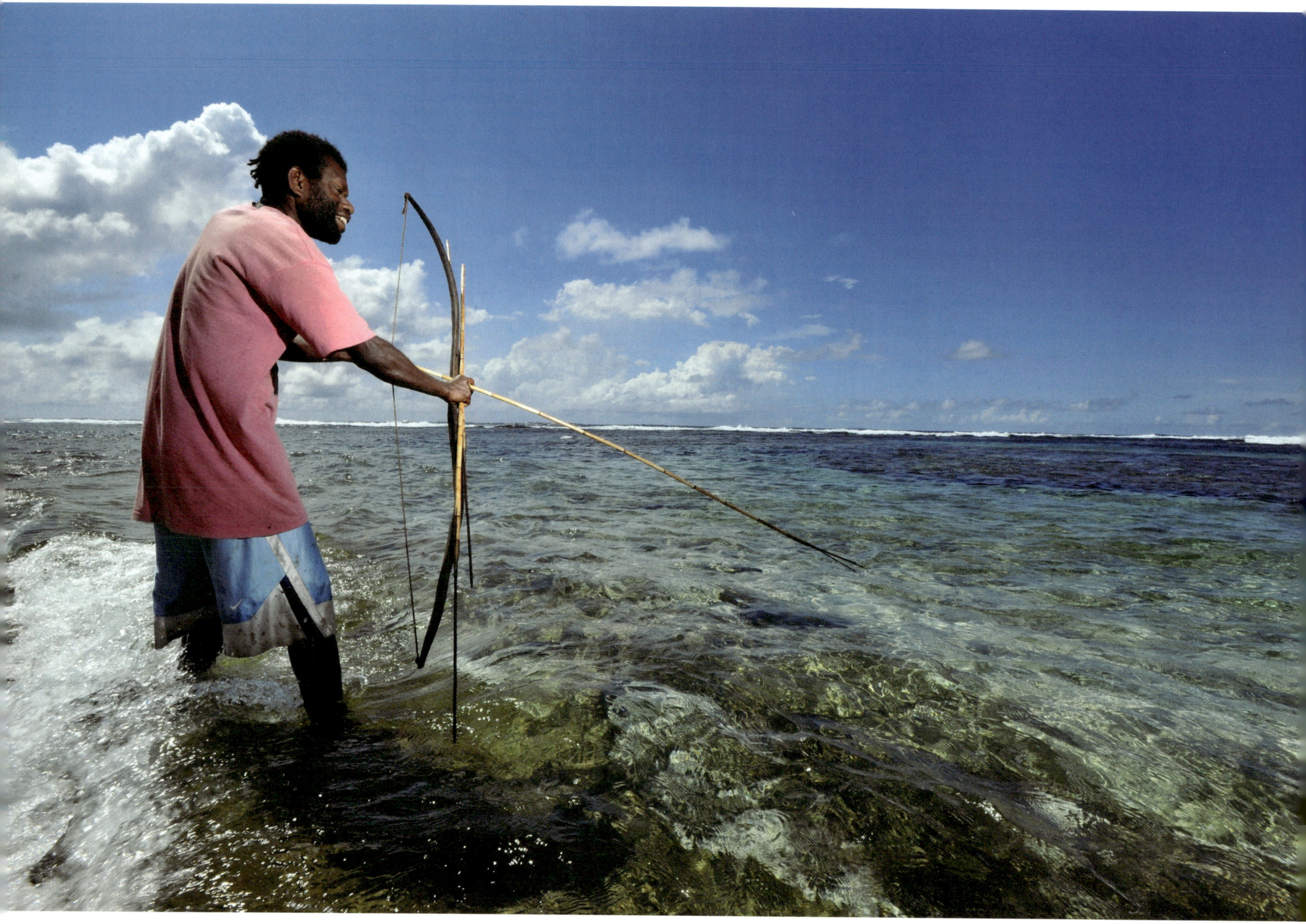

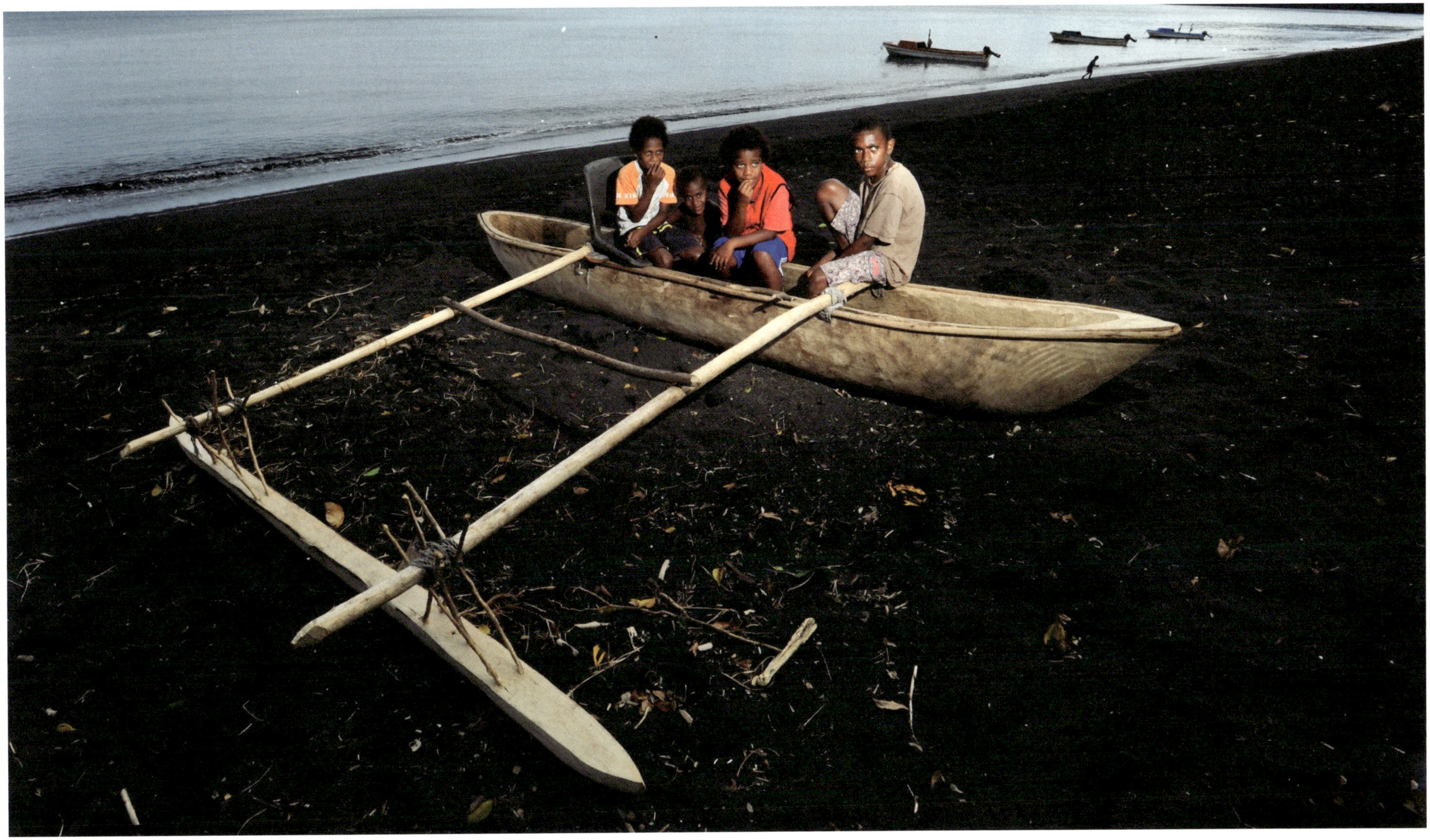

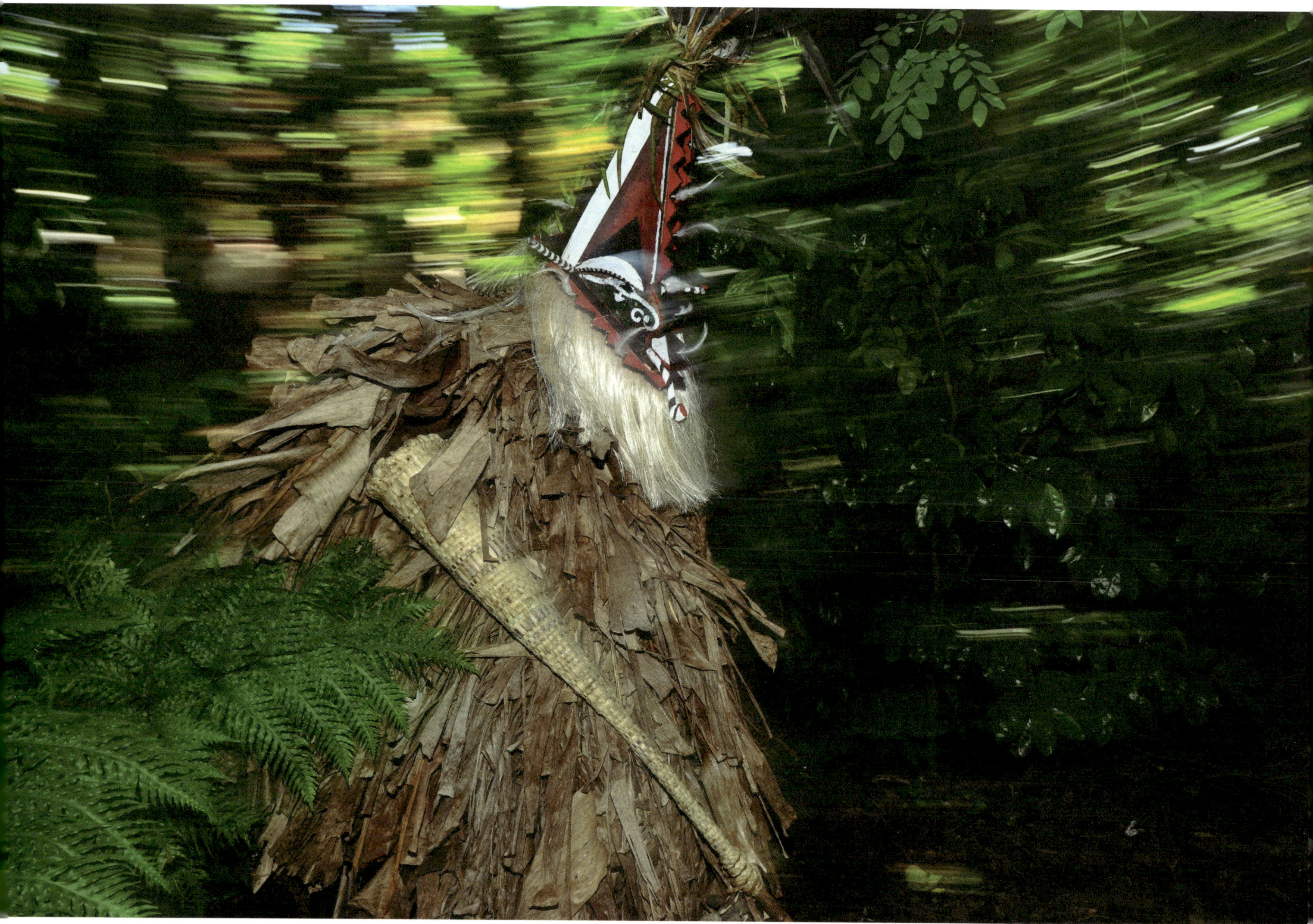

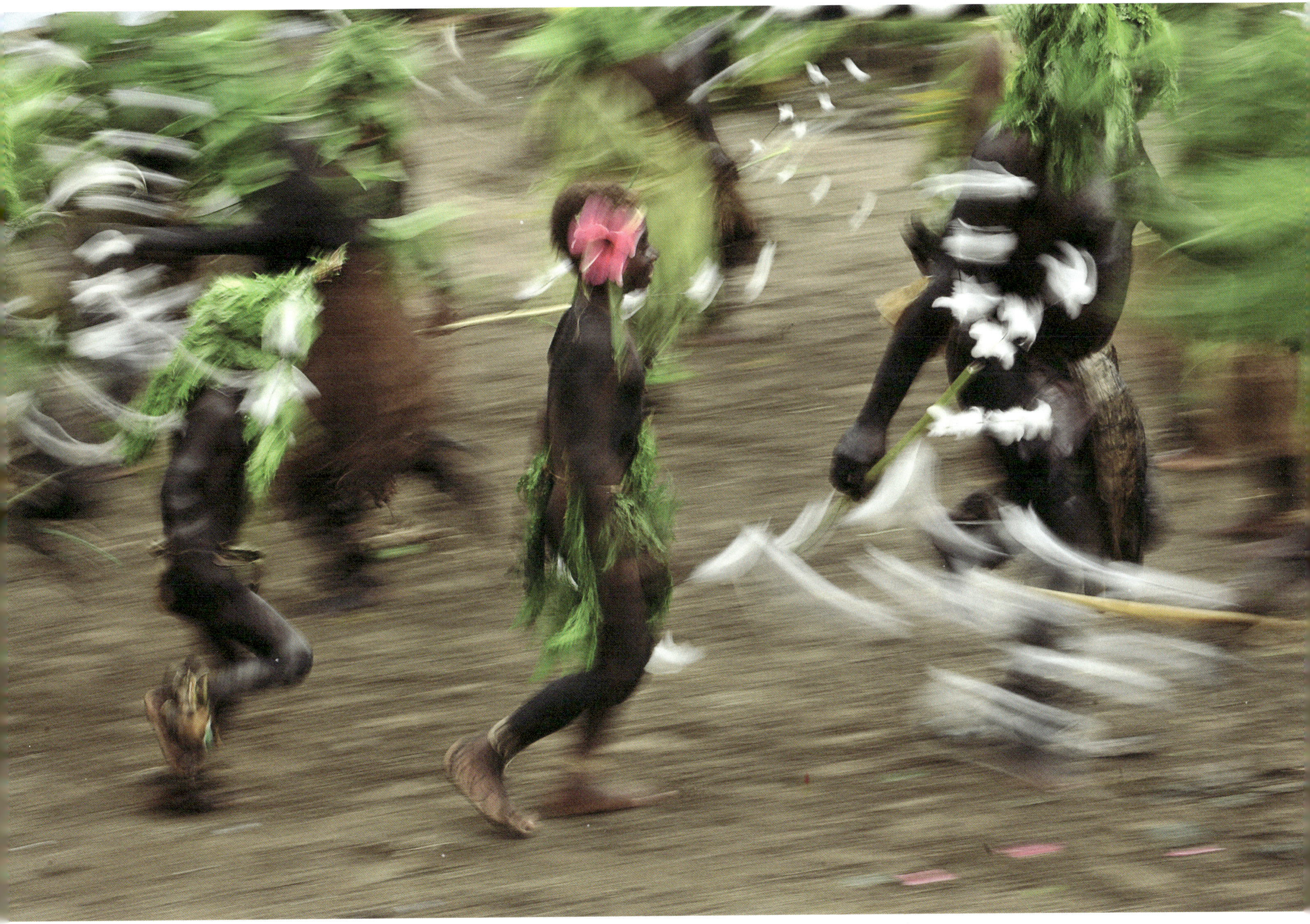

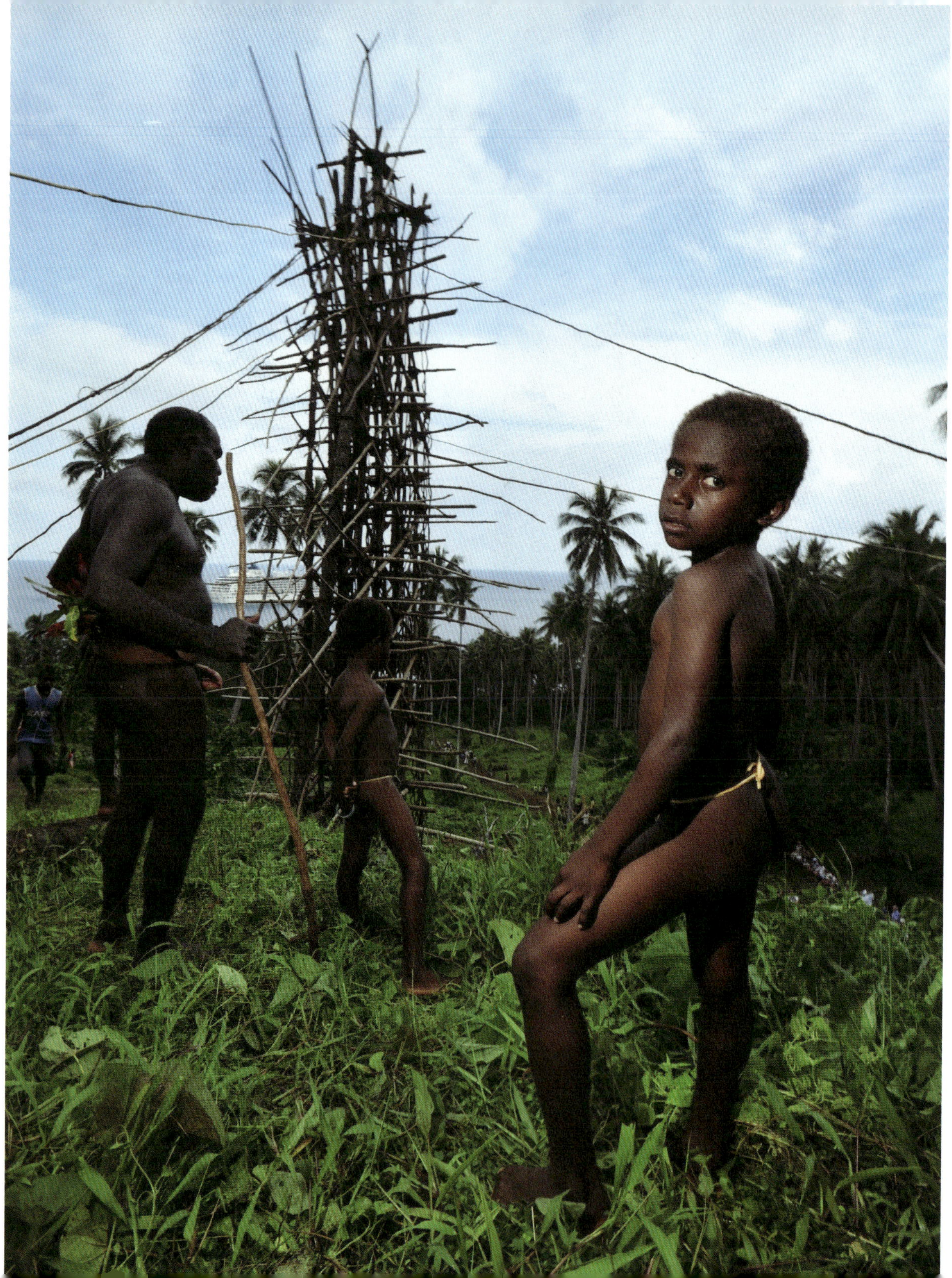

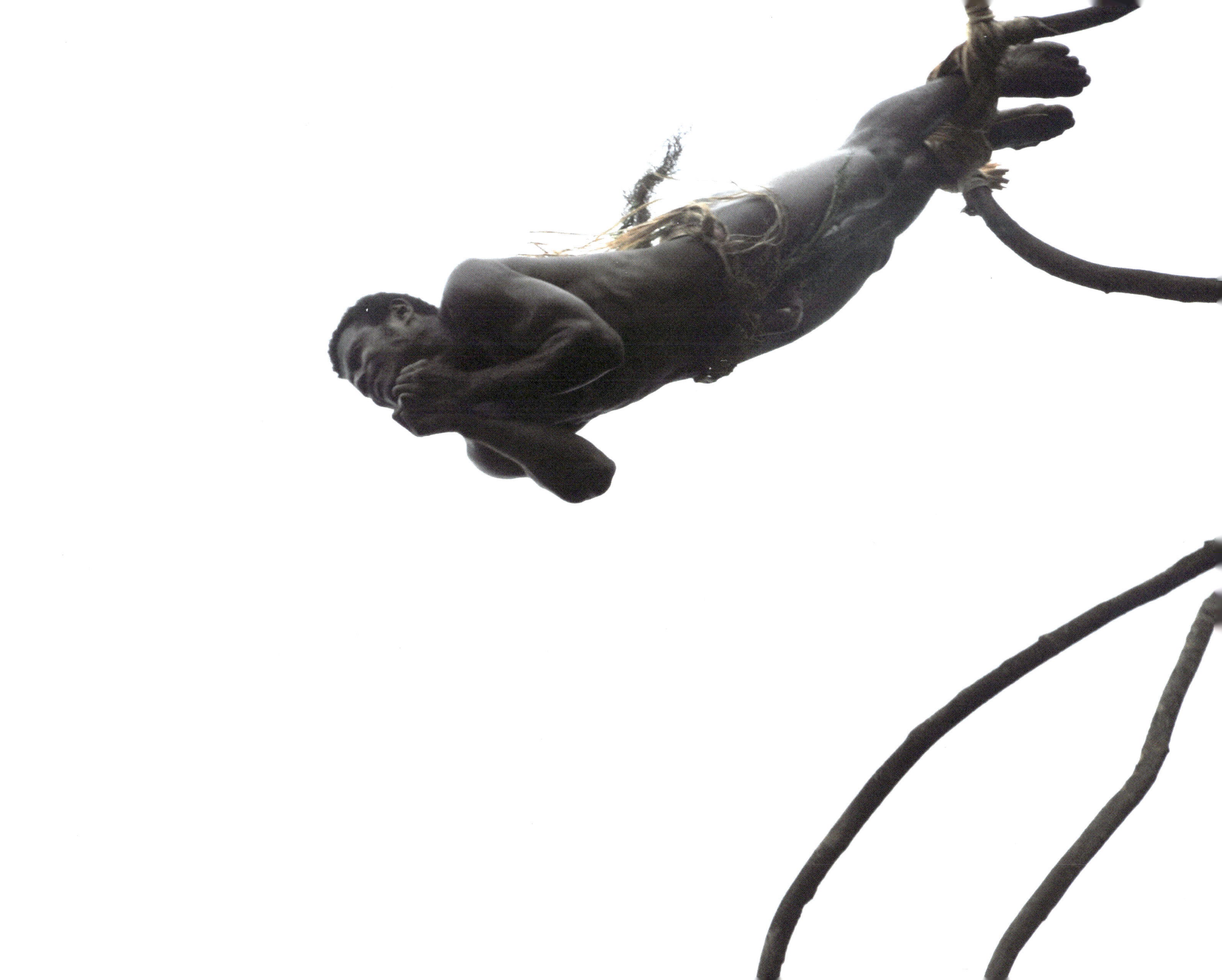

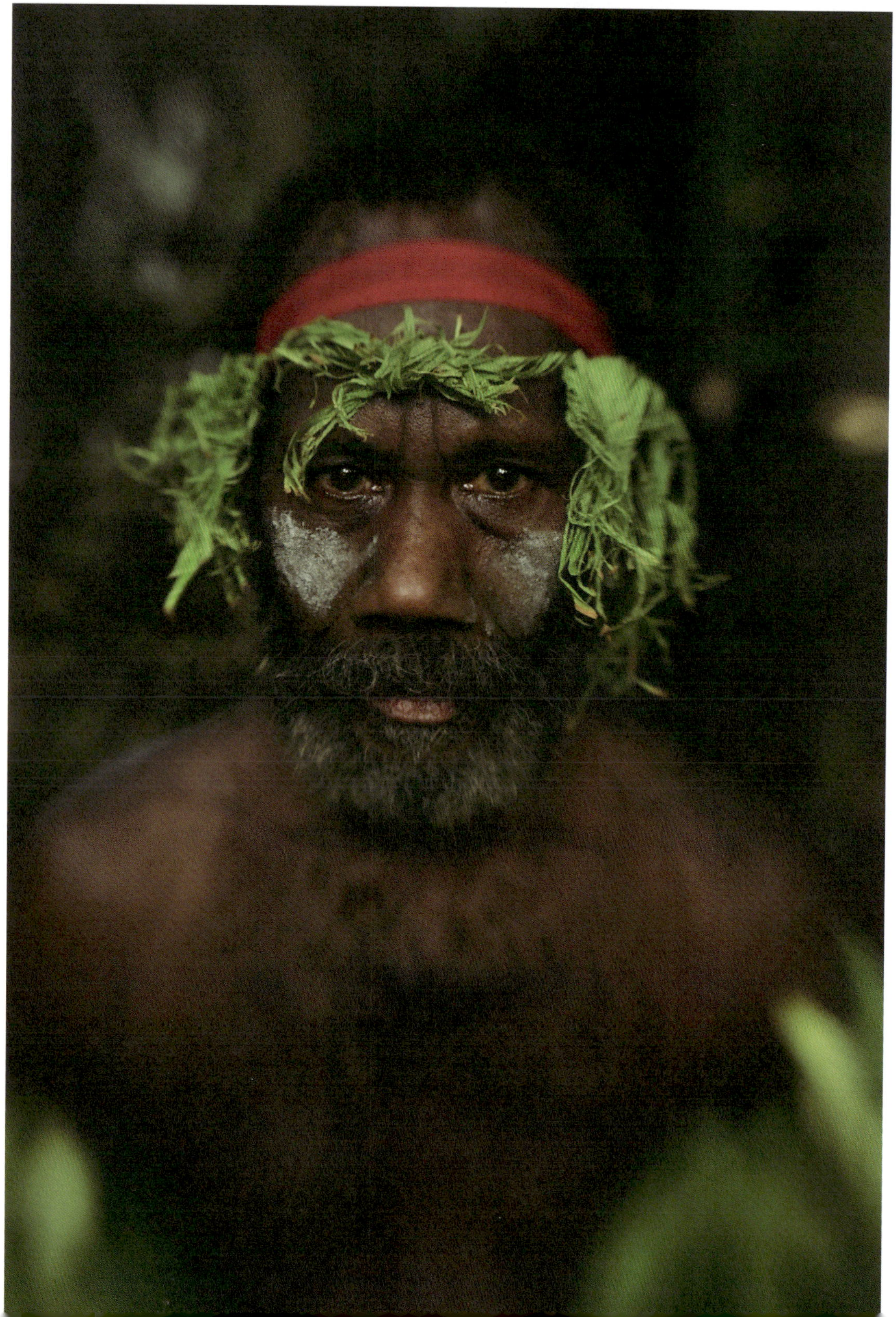

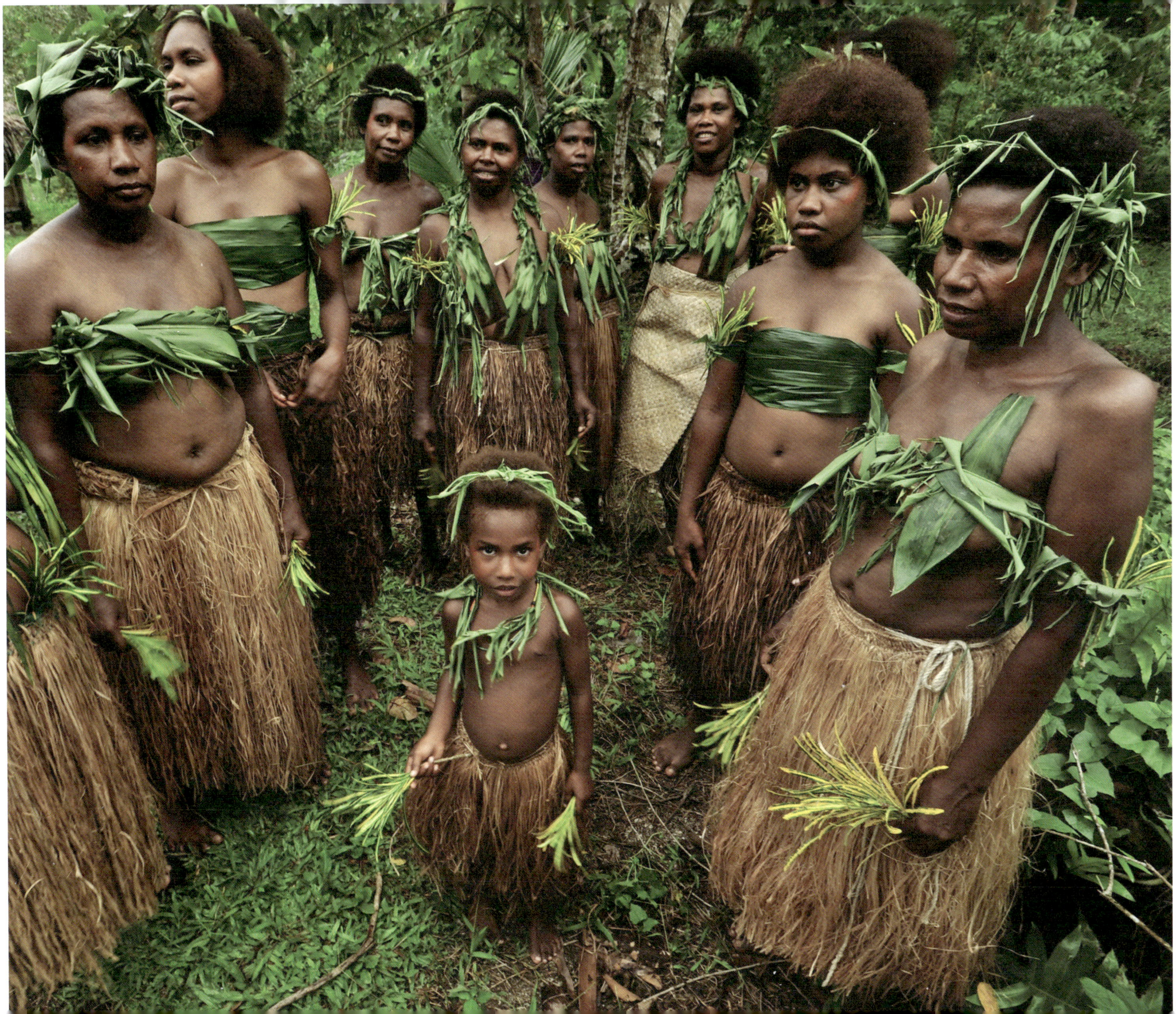

Chapter 5: Yield or Resist

The day of departure has arrived. The night before, I was kept awake by the comings and goings of the older men in the sleeping house, and with their snoring and smoking. It didn't help that my mind was continually conjuring up pictures of strange people and far away lands.

A cargo ship will dock at our pier of Ndui-Ndui later in the afternoon to pick us up. As no significant event in our lives passes without a feast, everyone will be at the pier later today. Excitement is in the air.

I'm walking away from Bumbu Joshua and everyone I love. I'm leaving behind my childhood and all that is dear to me. I close my eyes to feel how heavy my heart is. Even making my feet move takes great effort. But I'm also getting away from an illness that made me so weak I couldn't even walk. Thankfully, western medicines and Bumbu Janet's cooking gave me back my strength.

"Look at you, you've grown again!" exclaims Bumbu Celeste when I arrive at her hut to bid her farewell. She is sitting on a pandanus mat, weaving. "How I'd love to be with you all at Ndui-Ndui to see the boat come in." Her eyes look sad, full of regret that she can't walk anymore. It's an hour's walk to the jetty, and the whole village will be there to see us off.

"If we find someone to bring you back, I'll get you there in the wheelbarrow," I offer.

She's delighted. "Let's just go; they won't leave me there!" she laughs. I run to get our ride and lift her onto a cushion of folded mats. "I feel like a queen," she grins and holds on with both hands. An hour later, our thrill-ride ends. We arrive at the pier, just as a squall of rain drenches the congregation. I deliver Bumbu Celeste to her relatives and shake out my arms and hands.

Alain gets up. He holds out his prized knife. "Take my machete with you. You can't go away without one."

I blush as I think back to my ill-fated trip to the south of our island, and of my own bush knife that is rusting under some bush. Grabbing his well-sharpened blade, I thank him with a hug. My right hand is almost healed, but for one pesky sore spot that is still oozing. It and the gnarly red scar along my palm are covered by a freshly washed red bandage made from a t-shirt. I cradle the shaft in my hand, and while it still smarts, I feel good.

I start to polish my new bush knife with coconut oil and secretly wish Uncle Toka would offer me his ukulele, but he doesn't.

Music fills the air. Alain is playing the guitar, while his friend is strumming a ukulele. Dura has converted a tea chest into a bass by inserting a pole and tightening a metal wire onto it. He rhythmically plucks this string and produces a vibration that reminds me of all the happy evenings we spent singing and playing together.

The families of the "lucky" children are obliged to feed everyone in the village. Molrongo has offered up a goat as a brotherly gift and as a show of support for my education. It was slaughtered earlier and now hangs from the lower branches of the mango tree. Bumbu Joshua is preparing the spices for it – a mixture of wild ginger, turmeric and spring onions, all of which grow on the side of our taro patch.

I mill around the haka oven with Tari and cousin Toa, while Kwevira is busy working alongside the women. Lokin sits on his tail not far off and observes the excitement. He is anticipating the treats that will inevitably be thrown in his direction.

Mama Lovatu has collected some shorts and t-shirts and bought a new drinking cup and a mosquito net in the town of Vila. She even produced a "bras blong tut," a new green-handled toothbrush for me. I had hoped for a pair of shoes for the occasion, but there was not enough money for such a luxury. She wraps up a spoon and a knife in a towel that my older sister made for me.

Papa Viralongo calls me over. He pushes an envelope into my hands. "Here are some vatus for emergencies. You never know when you may need some funds. Take good care of the money, Abel," and with that, he folds me into a hug. I had not thought about money this whole time, but I am grateful and hide it in my backpack.

Bumbu Joshua takes me aside. "You have seen me read from this book," he says, holding on to his red leather-bound, well-worn Bible. He lifts it straight up to my heart. "Every question about life is answered in it."

We have often read verses and stories from the Scriptures together. I should perhaps know more of them by heart, but I hesitate to take the precious volume from him. He insists with a gentle nudge on my chest. I drop the machete and envelope the book, and both of his hands, with mine.

I worry about Bumbu Joshua. I don't know who is going to massage his knees or support him when he needs to walk somewhere or bring him his favorite food from the dining house. It has always been me.

The sun is now straight overhead and slightly to Uncle Toka's right, indicating that it is early afternoon and everything is happening on time, although some of the details still need to be finalized. On such occasions, Uncle Toka naturally assumes the responsibility of a coordinator, as is expected of uncles. He smoothly but decisively addresses the group of ladies who have assembled under the mango tree.

"Lara, send your boy to bring some more coconuts," he says as he scratches at his elbow. He squints, looking around, then asks, "Who's got a few more mats to sit on?" He loves being in charge, and everyone knows it.

Tari smirks as he points to Patrick. "Put the kava in the shade of the navele tree, Patrick," he commands, imitating Uncle Toka.

Tari's cousin, Paul Vula, strolls over to the food-laden table. His eyes are hidden behind a pair of mirrored sunglasses he brought back from town. He used to work on a cargo ship and has made several inter-island trips. He checks out the goat stew, chicken, fish, flying foxes, pork, eel and mud crabs, all cooked and brought to the feast by the women and guests.

Paul positions himself wide-legged before me, throwing his shadow on my face. "You're off soon," he smirks. "Enjoy being tossed about for eight straight hours on a cargo ship in the rough ocean."

Paul makes sure he is the center of attention, and everybody can hear him. Kwevira and Tari are certainly listening. I have only ever been a passenger on a dugout canoe, and that never went very far. I am not sure I really want to hear this.

"You'll sail from our port of Ndui Ndui to the port of Waterfall, nearest to Ranwadi High. There'll be nothing but sacks of cargo on that ship. If it rains, you get drenched, and if the sun scorches down, you fry."

"I'm not afraid of a bit of heat," I say, but a knot forms in my stomach. Although I stand close to one of the smoking ovens, I can sense huge rolling waves, and nausea is making me dizzy. I dislike how my face is reflected in Paul's dark sunglasses. If I walked away now, he'd think I was a coward. But I'm not a child anymore. I ball my hands into fists and squirm silently at the pain in my right hand. Paul leans towards me as if to challenge me. I wonder briefly if he is jealous, so I put my shoulders back and stand up tall.

"Ranwadi High sits atop a hill, above an anchorage of limestone boulders. From our ship, I could see the church hall with its giant cross and the buildings around it." Paul has everyone's attention, and he puffs himself up. "But there is a dangerous reef right at the port that has ripped open the hulls of many ships. They all sank, of course."

Paul swaggers to the haka and grabs a piece of chicken. He waves it before my nose. "Not much of that where you're going, I've been told," he says and takes a big bite.

Is he saying where I'm going there won't be enough food? I dismiss the thought. After all, he's just trying to get to me, but the idea doesn't want to be ignored.

"And once you are there, you won't be able to make sense of anybody's words, because everyone speaks their own dialect." With a lightning bolt in my stomach, I'm brought back to Paul's loud voice. *Is there no end to the bad news?*

I take a few steps away from my tormentor. As much as he wanted to leave, he was not chosen to attend high school abroad. He wants to be heard now, because he recently came back from a construction job far away. But what he's saying still bothers me.

"What do you mean? They don't even speak Bislama?" I ask.

"About as well as you do," Paul sneers. I blush, thinking about my recent failure.

"Some of these languages have never even been written down. But you will be taught in English, anyway. It will take you years until you can understand a real Englishman's talk. Trust me."

"OK, OK, I get it," I say, trying to end this conversation.

Vira, who has been listening, joins in. "I'm glad I'm not leaving after all. I never really enjoyed school anyway," he announces, to my great surprise. "If my parents hadn't made me go to school, I would have quit a long time ago. I'll spend another year or so in the village, then go to Santo, in Luganville Town, to see if I can find work in construction or in a hotel. I hear there are a lot of opportunities these days. I'll start making money soon, then come back and get married."

Vira's plan seems like a good one to me, and suddenly, I am jealous of him.

"I'd much rather live the life of a free-range rooster than be taught by white missionaries anyway!" he snaps decisively.

Vira's words make my heart miss a beat. I swallow hard. Panic rises in my throat, making my breaths shallow and ragged. I wish I could change places with Vira and continue the way I've always lived.

Paul starts again. "Missionaries from Australia and New Zealand have their ways of teaching you to follow their strict rules. You can't even use the latrines without asking permission," he adds, every one of his words adding to my agony. I glance around uneasily. He's enjoying my reaction, as every eye is fastened on us.

"Stop already!" I shout. I want to run, but I don't know where I'd go. I can't imagine being taught by white missionaries while living among strange people who speak strange languages and have strange customs. It makes me feel insignificant and powerless. The thought of having to submit to such torture for four years is too much to bear.

"Abel," I hear Bumbu Joshua's voice. I glance in his direction, and he beckons me. "The Good Lord has a plan for each of us. Will you let the words of others influence you? You know what you have to do. Now, go and do it!" His hand moves skywards to remind me of the Good Lord and the spirits of my ancestors. They will look after me.

Come with me, Bumbu Joshua, I think, and the silliness of this thought almost makes me laugh.

When the cargo ship finally arrives, the sun is touching the horizon. The whole congregation has been waiting for hours, and the excitement grows. Deckhands jump on land and secure the vessel with ropes before it gets dark. Waves crash against the wooden dock, foaming as they recede.

Don't make me go, my brain screams. My mouth, forced into a hard smile, says nothing. *You need someone who works in your fields and helps you with the harvest. You need someone who goes fishing for you. I can make your life easier.* He smiles at me.

My eyes plead with Bumbu Joshua as we make our way to the pier. He's holding on to my shoulder.

When we approach the cargo ship and its passengers, I count twenty-three boys and girls holding on to the railing. They must have boarded on other islands, but we all have the same destination. I look for sadness or excitement in their faces. Then I realize everyone's gaze is directed at one woman from our village. She enters the ship, balancing a bowl filled with lap-lap on her head and carrying jugs of water in both hands. She fills outstretched cups with water and hands out snacks. In the buzz around her, I don't understand a single word that is spoken.

"This is it." Kwevira is the first to put her foot on the gangway. Her mother and some relatives follow in the throng behind us.

"Move, Abel." Tari can't stand not being the first. He pushes past Kwevira and me. Then he leans over the railing to wait for his uncle and brother.

I step on the cargo boat in front of Bumbu Joshua and Dura. The sun has set, and darkness has fallen over all our activities. The odor of coffee, dried coconut and diesel fuel surrounds me like a cloud and threatens to cut off my breath.

Toa shouts from the pier, "I wish I could go with you!" But the voices from land become more distant as we get absorbed in the general activities on board.

"Study hard and make us proud," Bumbu Joshua squeezes my shoulder. He turns to leave me alone among the grubby sacks and the strange kids. Just then, a sudden swell almost knocks me off my feet, but I manage to grab hold of Bumbu Joshua. I want to hold on to him and take him with me, or better yet, leave the vessel with him. There could still be time. Then I think of Bumbu's mantra: *Nowhere else, with nobody else, doing nothing but this…* and I manage a short goodbye without crying.

The moment I drop my knapsack onto a pile of other bags, the captain sounds his horn. Kwevira has already said goodbye to her mother and watches her family leave. Tari is swinging his luggage like a pendulum, while one of his uncles doles out last-minute advice.

Finally, the three of us are alone. Most of the young passengers have gathered into small groups, chatting or resting on the deck. Kwevira, Tari and I stand close together at the railing. The distance between the pier and the ship widens. The moon and the stars throw a faint light on those we are leaving behind. We wave to them as they are becoming smaller and smaller. *Too far to swim now,* I think, and panic rises in my throat.

Kwevira is wiping her eyes with the back of her hands. I wish I could sit down and cry, too, but one look at Tari strengthens my resolve not to do that. Dread of the next few months fills my head until it is ready to explode. Nausea makes my stomach do somersaults. The three of us stand there, clinging to the rails like involuntary triplet ambassadors to a foreign land. I wish I could comfort Kwevira, but I can find no words to do so. Her company truly feels like a flower in the jungle to me, which is what her name means in the Ambae language.

Our beloved island fades into the distance, taking on the shape of a black, upside-down canoe with Lake Manaro in the volcanic crater at its peak. The ocean is a deep shade of blue, while waves crest and foam. It is going to be a long night.

Many of our fellow travelers are older, in their second or third year of high school. I keep a close eye on my knapsack. If I forgot anything, it's too late now. I strain my ears for some familiar words, while loneliness and sadness tug on my stomach.

A tall boy with short-cropped hair and fearsome eyes entertains his friends, broadcasting some information I wish I could understand. He's nestled atop a small mound of sacks he's arranged to serve as a bed, letting one leg dangle down lazily. Promptly, one of his friends gives the leg a kick. They laugh.

A girl with a tight ponytail relays a message to two other girls standing near her. The three are still savoring some of the lap-lap they received at our pier.

"Wanem nem blong yu?" One of the older kids points his chin in our direction. We are sitting among sacks of yams and coffee. Huge stalks of bananas and sugarcane surround us. It is dark, and the ocean is rough. With every swell our barge dives through, the spray of the waves sends showers over us. My hair is dripping, and my face tastes salty. The bandage over my hand is wet, making the wound sting.

"I'm Tari, and you?" Tari lifts his chin and looks the boy straight in the eyes. "Move over; there's space for two on this pile." He wipes a salty drip from his lashes, scales some sacks and plops down his knapsack, claiming a lofty seat. Then he looks down on me triumphantly.

My stomach wants to get rid of everything in it. I lie there limply, feeling sorry for myself. I am not in the mood for talking.

Kwevira takes a long look at me. She kneels down and without a word, lifts my left arm, turning the inside towards her. She digs three cold fingers into my arm just above the wrist. The pressure takes my attention from the nausea. I close my eyes.

"I learned that from my mother. It will help you feel better," she says matter-of-factly.

I want to thank her for helping me feel less alone, but my eyes and mouth stay closed. A sigh rises from my chest before I can suppress it. Pretty soon, the voices around us die down, and most of the youngsters nestle on or between sacks trying to find some comfort on this endless voyage.

If I had not taken this rusty old boat, I would not be suffering like this.

Kwevira now lifts my right arm and applies that same soothing pressure to my other wrist. Whether it is her kind gesture or my imagination, I do start to feel better. My stomach settles. I enjoy Kwevira's attention and care.

If I had not taken this voyage, I would not be experiencing this. It's definitely too dark to see that I'm smiling.

Chapter 6: Adapt or Perish

"We got a new truck!" shrieks a boy called Joachim, waking me up. I squint into the rising sun, then climb off the moist sack that was my bed for the night. Grabbing my knapsack, I join the kids at the railing who are scrambling to get a better look.

"Welcome to Waterfall," says a faded sign above the pier. High above the landing, cradled by lush jungle, lie a few white buildings.

This is magic, I think, as I realize with gratitude that this truck will bring us to our destination much faster than our feet.

Eagerly, we clamber off the barge and pile onto the truck bed. It turns out the older kids know where to situate their bony behinds so that the rough ride over the rutted roads is less painful and jarring. We newcomers, squatting on the rims of the truck bed, hold on with all our strength. We bump over a washed-out groove of lumpy coral. We ford a creek, splashing through a gurgling stream. The road is steep, and branches of bushes and trees whip our backs and faces. I study the tired scowls around me and wonder who might become a friend.

"Get your stinking feet off of me," my neighbor reprimands me. I understand his kick and wrinkled nose better than his words, as I try to regain my balance in a tight curve. I doubt we will be friends.

We arrive on a level area high above the sea. A gleaming white church and its surrounding smaller buildings greet us. *Just like Paul described it.* It looks like a whole village to me, built with brick and painted white. Nothing is thatched or freestanding like all of our homes in Hilvoliliu. Long rows of red, pink and white hibiscus plants look like they are standing to attention. Mango and breadfruit trees shade much of the area.

The gates open and the truck rolls into the courtyard. I grab my knapsack and jump off the truck bed. *Does the high and sturdy fence around the whole compound serve to keep the people in, or to keep dangers out?* After all, the land rises steeply into a mountain that is covered by dark forest. It looks impenetrable, ready to swallow up the man-made structures. I wonder if anybody has ever ventured into this wilderness, where lianas climb into the tree canopy and threaten to entangle trees and bushes – maybe even people. I straighten myself and take a deep breath despite my pounding heart.

Two big ladies dressed in blue missionary frocks divide the girls from the boys and lead us to our respective dormitories. The boys' dormitory is a two-story building to the right of the church. It looks out over the sea. Maybe it even looks out towards Ambae.

"What's the matter with your hand?" The older lady asks, pointing to the filthy bandage that is wrapped around it. The saltwater made the old gash ooze again. It is sore.

"Joachim, take Abel to the nurse." The matron picks the first boy who comes into her field of vision. Joachim tilts his head, motioning me to follow him. He seems to know the way well because we go straight to the nurse's station, which is in one of the teachers' houses. The door is locked. Joachim rings a bell, and soon a kind-looking lady in a white apron comes and sits me down inside, taking off the bandage.

"Ah, just a small wound left," she says in Bislama. "Quite badly infected, though."

Joachim peeks over her shoulder.

"What did you do to get such a deep cut? It seems like it is several weeks old already. No matter, I'll take care of it."

"Do you have dondakaya leaves here?" I ask. The nurse smiles and gets up, picking up a bottle with a brown liquid.

"I'll clean it with iodine," she says. "Don't scream now." Dark curls hide Joachim's forehead as he watches me. When the soaked cotton wool touches the infected spot, I want to not only scream but jump out the window. One look at Joachim, though, and I clench my teeth until they crunch. I inhale deeply. No sound comes over my lips. Joachim's eyes have not left mine. *Has he experienced something like this? Does he know how badly it hurts?*

I flash him a smile of relief when the pain subsides. He nods, returning my expression. He's a bit taller than I am and looks strong. He must be in the second year. He seems nice. *Could he be a friend in this place full of strangers?* I wish so with my whole heart.

"A bit of antibiotic cream will do the trick," the lady smiles and opens a tube. The iodine stung so bad that I don't even feel the cream. Then I get a fresh white bandage. "Come back tomorrow evening." She opens the door, and the two of us jog back to our dorms.

"Thanks for being there with me, Joachim." I wish I could think of more things to say, but we've reached our destination.

"You made me miss lunch," he says as an answer and saunters off to join his classmates on the upper floor of the building.

I am hungry, too. My stomach growls. But I have no food left, and there is nothing edible in sight. Not knowing what else to do, I slowly make my way into my dorm.

"Move, boy," I get shoved roughly as an older boy runs towards the belongings he had left here before the holidays. He throws his bag onto the top bunk and yells out to his friends. I search for Tari while I shove my few belongings into the bedside table. Thankfully, I see his backpack on the bottom bunk beside mine. Where is he? What do I do with my precious envelope? I open the drawer of the bedside table. *Too obvious.* Making sure nobody is watching me, I slide it under my mattress and then straighten the sheet again.

==//==

The afternoon passes in a flurry as we newcomers continue the tour through our new school. Grades seven and eight share one building, and grades nine and ten the other. We pass the dorms and arrive at a low building that holds a row of shower stalls and sinks. Above the doors, in a wavy line of red letters, it says, "I klinim gud." Behind that, we make our way to a row of toilet stalls, twelve latrines in all. Inside each cubicle is a cemented seat with a hole and a bucket. *Boy, does it smell awful around there.* I hold my nose and try not to breathe.

A bell startles me.

"Dinner time!"

I follow the throng that runs towards the dining hall. *Like a ravenous horde of pirates*, I think, while keeping pace with the pushing and shoving around me. Mangoes are piled in the center of a table in the center, and several bowls hold fried slices of taro. I secure my portion and take a seat.

"Hey, you sit over there," Lois points out a table where the new boys silently perch on the edge of their chairs. Then he invites Jonathan to sit beside him. I squeeze myself between two boys I don't know and search for Tari's face. He sits on the other side and has eyes only for his food. A pinch in my stomach threatens to take away my appetite. None of us are talking to each other. *How lonely one can feel in a room full of people.* I can't remember ever feeling this way before.

I look for Kwevira at the girls' table. She is chatting and laughing as if she was making new friends already.

I am here for a purpose, I remind myself. *I will become a teacher and guide for my clan. This is my reason for being here. None of these boys' destiny is to follow in the footsteps of my ancestors in our village.* Fortified with these thoughts, I peel my mango.

==//==

Later, we're streaming noisily into the dormitory. I look for Tari, who's making straight for his bunk. When I sit down on mine, I'm eager to tell him about my newly bandaged hand, but he's not interested in talking and puts his head on the pillow, facing away from me. I lie down, too, without sharing, and disappointed. I'd hoped we could be friends now that we're so far away from home. After all, Tari is the only boy I know. But he ignores me.

At home, Bumbu Joshua was interested in anything I wanted to show him. I clutch my stomach as the thoughts of strange teachers, unfamiliar classrooms and strict school rules wallop it. I swallow hard.

The lights go out, bringing a momentary hush over the room. After my eyes adjust to the dark, I can still make out the different colors of the bedspreads and various posters on the walls. In the men's sleeping house at home, it is a lot darker. *Bumbu Joshua, I hope you are okay without me!* The thought makes me so sad I want to cry.

I hear a lizard's padded feet as it scurries on the ceiling. Whispers and footsteps and other strange noises fill the night. There are sobs from some of the new arrivals.

"Jonathon is singing to his pillow." Out of the darkness, an unseen voice announces this to everyone in the room, surely making Jonathon's heart stop from embarrassment.

"There must be a piglet under Uranui's covers," says another, causing laughter all around. I like Uranui. He showed me his machete and slingshot earlier, and told me it took him three days on a cargo ship to arrive here from the most southern island of Tanna.

The windows are open. Night birds screech in search of food, and gusts of wind rustle in the branches of the trees in the yard. I let them transport me to Ambae. Although tears are already blocking my throat, I am determined not to cry. Curling up in a ball and putting my hands around myself, I rock back and forth. The longing to be home with my family overwhelms me.

I need to learn how to survive in this place full of strangers. My left hand draws comfort from Bumbu Joshua's soft red book under my pillow. As soon as the morning light comes up, I will read a chapter. Maybe it has a suggestion for finding a friend in a place like this.

Chapter 7: Rough Beginnings

The piercing sound of a bell wakes me up before dawn. For a moment, I am confused and don't know where I am. I take in the high ceiling and the breeze that blows freely through the door and the open windows. Two long rows of bunks fill the white-walled room, not leaving much space to move around. Unusual smells surprise my nostrils as I come up for air.

The strangeness of my surroundings hits me in the chest like a shot aimed at my heart, and I remember: it's my first school day at boarding school.

A nawimba bird sweetly answers the harsh wake-up call. *Back home last November, I watched the chicks hatching.* The memory sends a jolt of sadness through me. How I long for the thatch roof over our sleeping hut and the smoke from the cooking stoves that fills the morning air. I miss the sounds of our pigs, chickens and dogs competing with the song of the birds all around. Instead, sleepy boys stretch, grunt, and call out names in the early morning gloom.

I look at Tari, rolled up in his blanket in his bunk not three feet away. He seems to have slept through the blaring noise of the wake-up call.

"Hey, Tari, wake up," I say, still hoping to be friends in this place so far from home. Maybe he, too, was missing his family last night.

"Leave me alone," Tari mumbles as he pulls the blanket higher. Finally, he sits up and wipes the sleep from his eyes, but he doesn't look at me.

The big clock above the door shows it is 5:30. Allen Dan, a Form 3 boy and the head-boy of our dorm, enters the room.

"It's territory time! Out with you, you lazy lot," he shouts and expects everyone to jump onto the space beside the bed. "Stop loafing around and get your bums in gear. There are chores to be done before breakfast."

And with that, he thumb-tacks a large sheet of paper to the wooden door. Even though my Bislama is poor, his forceful tone of voice and his crude speech signal that he would not tolerate any nonsense from anyone. If only everyone here spoke Ambae, then the eagle Bumbu Joshua sees in me could fly a lot more easily.

I pull on my t-shirt and pad over to the door to inspect the list of chores that have to be done daily:

- Make the bed and clean up your stuff.
- Sweep the dormitories.
- Sweep the classrooms and chapel.
- Collect trash from the dorm, the classrooms and the school yard.
- Clean the showers and latrines.

My stomach growls, but I grab a bucket and proceed to our dorm's trash can. When I bend down to pick up a wrapper, I find Tari hiding under the bed. My first instinct is to yell at him, but what good would that do?

On my rounds, I find out that he's not the only one shirking his duty. Two boys from a higher grade play cards in the bushes near the library, out of sight of the teachers. It seems the older kids like to watch the younger ones toil, and I wonder why there isn't a teacher telling off the idlers.

The whole school ground is alive and buzzing in the light of dawn, with students dashing here and there. Some haul sloshing buckets, while others carry brooms, sponges and rags. The birds' early morning chorus is drowned out by kids yelling, laughing, screeching, and moving furniture.

At 6:30 sharp, the ear-splitting gong puts an end to the activities, announcing shower time, followed by breakfast. There we find strange items on the tables: pieces of bread, marmalade and milk-coffee. I pine for the fried breadfruit Bumbu Janet would always prepare for me before school.

The big clocks in the halls and the jarring sound of the bell regiment our day, calling us to hurry here and there. The corridors are like a swarming anthill.

Older students stride purposefully to their classroom doors. I don't know what to expect. I look for Tari and Kwevira, but they are already crowding through the classroom door. I feel rushed as all the students pick their favorite desks. The noise around me is deafening. I choose the empty chair beside Uranui, whose eyes are riveted to a marking on the table. Is he as nervous as I am? The moment I slide into my seat, the room falls silent.

A short, somber-looking man enters and strides towards the front desk. He hits it twice with a baton. One could have heard a lizard breathing.

He writes his name in large letters on the blackboard: Mr. Wilson, Headmaster. The scratching of the chalk makes my hairs stand on end. His balding head sports a ring of white curls. *Curls like Bumbu Joshua.* The thought makes me miss my family so badly I want to cry.

Then I remember Joachim telling a wide-eyed audience of newcomers that our headmaster once locked a student into a small closet all night for making noise in the dorm. I pray I never get on the wrong side of him.

"Good morning, class," Mr. Wilson's deep voice quickly brings me back to reality. He looks at every student, using his baton to underline the words he says.

"A boarding school like this needs strict rules. Obviously, all students are to stay within the fence at all times, except if they have special permission to leave on weekends.

"If you are caught breaking a rule, you will be punished. Detention on Saturday is just one of these punishments, and too many detentions will result in expulsion."

When Mr. Wilson speaks, the veins on his neck bulge. The button on his dark suit jacket is straining to keep the garment closed over his big belly. I half expect this button to pop with the next deep breath he takes.

"You are here because you were a good student in your village. Do not take this lightly; you will have to prove yourself at this school. Not everyone will still be here next year. Those who do not give their very best, and those, whose results lie in the lowest percentile, will be sent home. Always remember the great sacrifices that were made to allow you to be here.

"You will get an education so you may achieve great things. In return, I expect absolute obedience from each one of you in order to achieve that goal."

In this room full of students, not a whisper can be heard. A shiver runs down my spine. *How could I ever think I was made for this kind of life? A life of rules, without the ability to ever roam free or to decide what I want to do.* I wonder if I can get the next cargo ship back to Ambae.

But then I remember how sick I was on that ship. And what hopes Bumbu Joshua has for me, and what sacrifices it took for him and many others who have worked so hard to get me here.

What else has Mr. Wilson been saying? The sound of scraping and sliding chairs hauls me back to this classroom.

"All rise and welcome Mrs. Lawrence, your English teacher from Great Britain." And with that, he turns to leave.

A pale lady enters, her skinny frame wrapped in a grey skirt. Her light brown hair is tied in a knot at the back of her head, and big glasses sit atop her nose. She nods to Mr. Wilson without so much as a smile while her bony fingers fiddle with a pen. *Maybe there is not enough food in Great Britain,* I think and feel a bit sorry for her.

"What is your name?" she asks each of us, one after the other, in a high voice. Students begin to answer as she points to them, and one by one, my turn approaches. My heart beats hard.

"My name is Abel. I come from Ambae," I manage to say before my face turns red and I hastily sit down again. But the chair has vanished and I find myself sprawled on the floor, feet in the air. Sniggers all around make it hard to get up. I am so embarrassed I want to disappear. I look back and see John, the boy behind me, laughing and looking at me with a taunt, and I understand.

"My name is Kwevira, and I am also from Ambae." Mrs. Lawrence has turned around and is continuing her questioning at the front of the next aisle. Has she not noticed anything?

"The English language is spoken by more than a billion people all over the world. After four years at this school, I hope that will be one billion and thirty-one." Her mouth keeps moving, but my attention is elsewhere. I don't catch a lot of what she says that day.

I have a score to settle with John, and I am planning revenge. He doesn't speak my language, and neither of us can communicate yet in English. What I plan to make him understand, though, does not need words. If he thinks he can make me a laughing stock on the first day of school, he is wrong.

Geography is the last class of the day. Our teacher, Mr. Mangau, is not much older than my brother Molrongo. His hair is shaved above the ears, leaving the crown in a tight frizz of dark curls that he likes to comb with his fingers. He does not move through the class but sits at his desk, looking happy with himself.

For the first time in this day full of new sensations, I relax a bit. A big map of Vanuatu hangs over the blackboard, the archipelago of 84 islands making a vague heart shape in the vast expanse of the Pacific Ocean. I, at least, know where Ambae lies.

"For many years, French and British powers called our islands 'New Hebrides'. When did Vanuatu become a republic?" our teacher asks, speaking Bislama.

I don't speak Bislama well, but I understood the two important words of his question. My hand shoots up. "Kantri hem i winim independens long 1980!" I shout without regard to the others. Mr. Mangau points a finger at me and tells me to wait until I am called. I glance at Tari. *Beat you,* I smile.

Soon after, we get up and sing our national anthem: "Yu-mi, Yu-mi, Yu-mi" or "We, We, We." Bumbu Joshua and I, both proud Ni-Vanuatu, often sang it together.

And then comes the moment I've been waiting for. John gets called to the blackboard to point out the island he comes from. I make myself look busy as he returns to his desk. When his front leg lines up beside me, I put out my foot, and he promptly falls over it, crashing against his desk. His chair falls to the ground with a few bounces. Mr. Mangau lifts his head and assesses the scene.

"Abel Nako, are you the cause of this ruckus?" His eyes rest on me. A jolt shoots through my stomach. I am not prepared for the hurt that disappointing my favorite teacher causes me. "Put your name on the list for detention. That will be on Saturday in two weeks, because next Saturday is already full."

Keeping my head low, I take a pen and add my name to the two already on the list. *Nice impression to make on the first day!*

I soon learn that Saturday detention means working in the heat for hours, cutting bush grass or weeding the gardens. I sigh. But inwardly my heart skips a beat. John is wiping blood from a cut on his lip. I am satisfied with myself. Bumbu Joshua had once said to me, "Every step you take and every action you undertake is supported by a thousand ancestors." I feel my great-great-grandfather smiling down at me for standing up for myself. It makes me walk taller. I'm confident that John will not bother me again.

==//==

Saturday is supposed to be our free day. We have neither school nor church services, only territory time, as we do every day. Last week I organized my school folders and assignments, enjoyed browsing through the books at the library, and then joined a ballgame in the yard. But today, I have to report to Mr. Mangau, who's waiting in Classroom 7. He stands by the door, ticking off our names on his list of convicts. Every one of them had been publicly announced in a student assembly the previous day.

Ricky and Silas from Form 3 enter right behind me. They don't seem overly concerned about having to toil in the school grounds for three hours. How I envy their camaraderie! They had been caught cutting Sunday Combine service at Lalwori village last Sunday and went fishing instead. I, on the other hand, fear for my reputation. What if Bumbu Joshua hears about this? How many more of these punishments before I get sent home in shame? I couldn't bear the disgrace.

Mr. Mangau leads us to a large patch of hard, unruly jungle grass of the bamboo family. The main focus of these punishments, I sense, is to draw attention to the lawbreaker and cause him humiliation. Gossip about me has already started. Tari made a bet with Rodney, saying that I would surely faint in half an hour, since I was not used to do such strenuous labor in the blazing sun.

Those who are free can watch us toil with our machetes. They have even stopped tossing a ball to shout useless advice. This is as embarrassing as it is annoying.

"Whack it harder, Abel!" Tari's voice gloats. I pretend not to hear.

"Crouch, don't stoop!" *Thanks for the good advice, Joachim. I'm sure you've practiced that a few times yourself.* I wipe the sweat that runs down my neck, leaving dusty streaks.

"Try pulling it out with your hands!" Even without looking up, I know this stupid remark is Rodney's. Why are these guys so mean?

"You obviously have experience. Get stuffed, dumbhead," I say, feeling somewhat protected by the two sixth-graders working alongside me. I had actually tried pulling up the bamboo shoots at the beginning, but the tightly packed earth does not give up the roots of this plant easily. The jungle always tries to take back any land that was wrested from it.

I am so thirsty! Every exposed bit of skin itches. A blister is forming on my hand just where the scar from my cut ends. I contemplate praying to God and my ancestors, promising never to misbehave again. But I really don't feel like adding the accusation of being a liar to the ones I am shouldering already. Surely their wrath would cause a much harsher punishment than this.

When Mr. Mangau's whistle signals that my time is up, I wipe the sweat off my face and hurry to the showers. I hear Bumbu Joshua's voice asking me what I have learned from this. *Never to get caught again,* is my silent answer.

After the shower, hunger and thirst drive me back into the courtyard. Tari is telling a story, and Joachim and Rodney laugh. *It's most likely something embarrassing about me,* I think, though maybe I'm just being paranoid. Will I have to live in fear of these boys every day? Summoning all my courage, I decide to approach them.

"Hello," I say brightly. *Please be kind to me,* I want to add, but they look at each other and burst out laughing.

"Look, he wants to talk to us," they snort. *Wow, that stings.* At a loss for what to do, I turn and walk about aimlessly, rubbing the big blister on my hand.

I am still mad when the lunch bell rings. After this awful morning, I have kitchen duty. I'm not sure I can bear this life much longer. I let myself sink into a dark pit of loneliness. At least I'm working with Uranui today.

"I smell fish!" he shouts and chucks the ball underhand into the courtyard, ending the game he was playing.

No doubt, it's cabbage soup again, I think, yet I speed up my step because I look forward to anything that fills my stomach. We enter the cooking shed, inhaling the smoky aroma deeply. The long trough on the ground is filled with firewood, spewing sparks left and right. Above it simmer two huge cauldrons of soup and two of sweet potato.

Uranui and I fetch steel bowls and position them beside the cauldrons on the ground. The cook, a big lady in a missionary dress, fills the pots. Then we lug them, one by one, into the dining hall and put one bowl on each of the twelve long tables. Kitchen duty is good, I smile, as we both choke down a piece of sweet potato on our way to the kitchen before we get the next bowl. We are partners in crime, and it feels good.

Everyone is lined up outside the door, armed with a bowl and a spoon. A teacher opens the door, and the hungry horde spills in, girls to one side and boys to the other. I hurry to my table, too, so that I'm not the last to dish up my share. After the other boys have served themselves, I am lucky if my ladle comes out filled to the top.

"Could I please have another bowl of cabbage soup?" I beg the cook as she walks by. "Even my little brother at home eats more food than this!"

"There was exactly enough for eight," is her answer. I scrape out what is left in the pot with my fingers. *I'm still hungry*, I want to scream. Nobody looks at me. Every boy's face is turned towards his portion while he's wolfing it down fast. *Each man for himself,* I think as my stomach aches with hunger and foreboding. *Bumbu Joshua, this is not what you have taught me.*

After we have scrubbed our bowls and utensils with coconut husks under a tap outside, many boys spend the afternoon playing soccer. The girls prefer to play volleyball, watch the soccer game, or chat in small groups. I choose the quiet of the library where I can study for Monday's English test. For a moment, I contemplate opening the closet and borrowing Mr. Mangau's guitar. Strumming the cords would take the sting out of my misery. Yet my greatest motivation is to beat Tari in the English test, so I pull an English workbook from the shelf and start filling out one of the exercises.

The door opens. When I look up, I am confronted with the broad nose and short-cropped hair of Rodney. He's looking for mischief; my heart sinks. *This cannot be good,* my mind screams and tells my feet to run. But I stay nailed to the chair, concentrating on the phrases in front of me. Rodney's friends Ho'okano and Luke saunter into the room.

"Too poor for your own books?" Ho'okano's voice drips with pity. His name means "proud", and he is. A tight yellow t-shirt accentuates his muscles and a golden chain around his neck sparkles. His frizzy hair is tied back with a rubber band.

"Don't make the books dirty with your filthy little fingers," Luke adds, his mousy face close to mine. He's smaller than I am, but together with his big friends, he can give free rein to his cruelty. *One day I will get you alone, and I will make you beg for mercy,* I swear to myself. This bubble is burst by Rodney, who yanks the precious book from my grasp.

He holds it up and slowly rips out a page, then another, his eyes fastened on me.

"What exactly did you call me this morning?" he asks, then he flings the book towards me. Its spine hits first my head and then the floor. My pulse rushes in my ears and pounds in my temples as Rodney approaches the table, steps behind me and pulls out the chair with me on it. Then he tilts it until I fall to the floor.

"Let this be a lesson to watch your mouth when you talk to me, shrimp." And with a final kick in my backside, the three back off.

"Tearing pages out of public property, tsk, tsk. Maybe we tell Mrs. Lawrence what you did. That might get you another detention," Ho'okano says, and the three laugh all the way out the door.

I stay where I am for a moment, then scramble to my feet. The torn pages lie crumpled under the table. If I pick them up and use them, it will look as if I tore them from the book. I fold them up and put them in my pocket. Then I slide the book back on the shelf.

==//==

Nightbirds screech and cicadas click and chirp, but all I can hear is the growling of my stomach as I lie in bed and wait for sleep.

I'm so hungry I could eat a whole pig! My fantasy takes me home to Ambae. *What I would give for a wood pigeon, perfectly roasted over a fire.* The thought makes my mouth water. It conjures up pictures of Sunday feasts with my family. Here, we have not seen meat since last Sunday, and even then, I only ended up with two meager pigeon wings. Two other times we had a few shreds of canned fish in our vegetable stew.

Hunger gnaws at our bellies every day, and it interferes with my thinking and learning. How can I concentrate on historical facts when my stomach growls? How can I memorize vocabulary when my head hurts? How can I remember mathematical formulae when all I can think of is Bumbu Janet's roasts?

I know I won't be able to sleep for the rumbling in my stomach. Reluctantly, I slide my hand under the mattress. I search for the envelope and silently pull it out. My fingers tenderly stroke the bundle of vatus, then I pick a few of the notes and dig them deep into the pocket of my shorts. Carefully, I replace the envelope in its hiding place. *This is an emergency, Papa Viralongo,* I defend myself.

Then, pretending to use the latrines, I make my way to the canteen. My mouth salivates at the display of assorted biscuits, tinned foods and sweets of all sorts.

I buy a packet of cream crackers and hide them in my shorts. Then I sneak back into the dorm. It's hard to wait until total darkness while my stomach is doing somersaults. But finally, when all has gone quiet, I unwrap the treat under my blanket, hoping the crackling paper will not give me away. If Tari hears what I am doing, he will beg one off me. Hiding under my covers, I demolish the crackers one by one.

CHAPTER 8: THE HUNT

"I'd love to chew on roasted coconut right now," I share with Kwevira at break time in the courtyard, while we sit together in the sun.

"My favorite is chicken wrapped in banana leaves and baked on hot stones," she continues our daydream. "With sweet potato," Kwevira licks her lips.

"Hey, Bunbun Karong!" Joachim is walking by with a few of his classmates. My face lights up. He's speaking to me, calling me "Bony Fish." Some of the boys laugh. But he leaves the group and comes towards me. Then he whispers in my ear, "You want to go hunting with me?"

Hunting? Why is he inviting me? As an offering of friendship? I can't help but salivate as images of roasted wood pigeons and fruit bats appear in my mind.

It is late afternoon, and nobody pays attention to me as I amble towards the latrines, where I have agreed to meet Joachim. My heart is pounding for fear of getting caught, and also for the sheer excitement and anticipation of shooting and picking my own food.

Near the smelliest part, Joachim points out a piece of chain-link fence that is hanging loose. It gives us barely enough space to wiggle through, but we do, and after a few steps, we find ourselves inside the thick jungle that surrounds our school on three sides.

Pandanus trees show off their beautiful fruit pods, but they are not for eating. A wild avocado tree tempts me. I pick a few of the hard fruit, knowing they are still inedible. Looking around for a hiding place, I choose a large banyan tree with a hollow in its roots. There I hide our loot and await its ripening.

Coconut palms reach to the sky. Joachim fastens the machete around his waist and scales one of the trunks in seconds. Two green fruits fall to the ground. With the help of a dead branch, I tear open the coconut husks while he climbs down.

I bet I could have done that just as fast, I think as I drink the delicious liquid. It's so refreshing! Juice runs down our chins and stains our t-shirts. Three more hacks with Joachim's knife, and the shell opens to let us scoop out the soft meat. Then we abandon the empty shells and go looking for prey.

"How good are you with this slingshot of yours?" Joachim points at my weapon with his chin. He has already proved his skill with the machete. He needlessly whacks at a bush with his knife, and its branches fall to the ground.

Birds screech and hoot all around us. The droning of cicadas fills any silences. Then a shrike bird alights not ten feet from us. I remember what Bumbu Joshua taught me: *become invisible.* Except for my wildly beating heart, I become silent, still as a tam-tam at night. My slingshot is ready to fire. When a fly buzzes around my left ear, I do not shoo it away.

I crouch down. With steady fingers, I tighten the rubber on my weapon and wait for the right moment. The bird is in no hurry and calmly pecks at some invisible seeds on the ground.

Turn just a bit. Yes, a bit more…

The pebble screams through the air, and the bird never knew what hit it. I proudly run towards it and wring its neck as I have often watched Bumbu Joshua do. Now I need to slit open its belly and clean out whatever is loose in the cavity.

"I need your machete for this," I proclaim and offer my trophy to Joachim. "Hey, Joachim, where are you?" No answer. I wonder what he's up to and look behind some of the bigger trees near me. Nothing.

"If you are joking, this isn't funny," I shout, but a quaver has crept into my voice. I fear that time is getting short. I do not want to get caught. "Let's go back now," I say, almost pleadingly. My heart is pounding in my ears and drowning out the screeches of the birds. The trees cover the whole view of the sky. I am not sure I can find my way back to our entry point by myself.

I grab a few ripe bananas from a banana tree and peel one. What if I have to spend the night out here? Will I be mauled by a creature? Will I fall prey to a spirit? Will I be expelled from school? My heart is on such a crazy dance that I can't even think straight. I tuck my t-shirt into my shorts and pack a few more of the sweet treats, just in case.

What direction did we come from? I kick myself for not paying attention. The whole time I wanted to impress Joachim, but now I have no idea where he is. As a precaution, I lay a bright yellow banana peel under the tree nearest me. I walk 100 steps one way, trying to recognize a stump, a plant, a distinctive tree. Nothing. Back to the peel. I walk in a different direction. There must be something I recognize, but I can't say for sure. Tears force themselves into my eyes, and I don't even attempt to swallow them down.

Getting tricked by Joachim makes me as angry as it makes me sad. I thought he wanted to be a friend. This stings, and brings back my loneliness with a force that throws me to the ground at the foot of a banyan tree. There I rest, dejected and glum.

The sun will be setting shortly. It's time to gather my wits. I had been hungry, and another student pretended to be my friend. I trusted him, but he betrayed my trust and lured me into the forest labyrinth to abandon me there. I voluntarily broke school rules and left the grounds without permission. I'm not sure who is more to blame, Joachim or I.

With a jolt, I realize that if I want to get out of here, I can only depend on myself. I am the one I must be able to count on. *My life is not only a series of things happening to me – but I am also happening to the world. I am a force to be reckoned with!* This thought is new and fills me with power. Thank you, spirits that live in the banyan tree.

I walk stealthily in the one direction away from the banana peel I have not gone yet. What if this is still the wrong way? I'm counting my steps…79, 80, 81…

Hey, there is the bush Joachim decapitated! Its branches are strewn uselessly onto the ground. Or, most usefully, I rejoice and thank the spirits that are looking out for me. The sun is taking her light away, and I stumble over a root I had not seen. Sorry, left knee. Sorry, bananas in my t-shirt. Nothing matters, because I am on the right path.

There, a rooster dashes past me, followed by two hens. *What a great meal they would make.* At this time, though, I don't dare to act on this impulse. I have put my slingshot back in the left pocket of my shorts. Killing a wild bird is one thing, but killing somebody's rooster is quite another. *What do the laws of an island like Pentecost say about this matter?*

I don't even know whose territory I am in, but I know the landowners of the Lalwori tribe do not take kindly to thieves. Getting caught on somebody's land may spell great trouble not only for me but also for the school. I feel so small out here, so unprotected, and with every passing moment, more like a sitting pigeon awaiting its shot to the heart.

I lay my hand onto the bark of one of the giant banyan trees and promise my ancestors I'll be more careful next time. Then I let the few dim lights from our school point the way for me in the sudden night. It all looks so different in the darkness. Not long after, the stench of the latrines irritates my nose. With a sigh of relief, I grope along the fence to find the part that allowed us to steal away. When a loose wire catches my shorts, I crouch down and wiggle back into safety.

Thoughts of what is awaiting me make my pulse hammer in my temples. My heartbeat almost chokes me and makes it hard to breathe.

When I come back, the halls are quiet. I meet nobody as I sneak into the deserted dormitory. There, I fish out the harvest of bananas from my t-shirt. I lay one under Tari's pillow and one under Uranui's. And I keep one to give to Kwevira in the morning.

Then I make my way to assembly, hoping to join in unnoticed. But I'm ready to face any punishment I may have to endure, no matter how harsh. Even if I am sent home on the next cargo ship, I will endure it. Nonetheless, the shame of it makes my face hot.

As I rejoin my classmates, they are hanging up new chore sheets. I look interested and nonchalantly join a small group near the door. I wring my hands as if they were wet from washing. Individual students complain about the cleaning jobs assigned to them, while others huddle and make plans for how to speed up some of the chores. Tari sits on a bench and reads a comic from the library. Nobody pays attention to me, except Joachim, who throws me a surprised glance. *I will get you back for this*, I swear under my breath.

Even though he didn't mean to, he did me a favor, I realize. He has emboldened me to find food without having to pay for it. Thanks for that, Joachim. I straighten up and stare right back at him. *I will go out there again, but not with you, you traitor.*

Chapter 9: Black Magic

After dinner one night, we gather for worship in the chapel. I remember to wash my hands before I grab Bumbu Joshua's precious red Bible and join the others who file into the pews.

I love it when some of the older kids play the ukulele, accompanying Mr. Mangau on the guitar. Today we sing a new hymn. I hear "Their Snowman Like Jesus" and I remember a geography class where we learned that rain in the northern hemisphere may fall as white snow. I know Jesus, of course, but nowhere in the Bible have I heard about Jesus being a snowman.

Our pastor, Father Ephraim Vuti, is a little man, but his voice is that of a giant. His curly hair is disheveled, and streaks of white do nothing to restore order on his head. But his face is kind, and he seems to have an open ear for our concerns and questions.

I raise my hand. When invited to speak, I ask, "I wonder what a snowman is?" Father Ephraim looks stumped for a moment. I am confused: isn't he supposed to know these things? Then his face breaks into a big smile.

"There's NO man like Jesus, Abel, that's what we are singing." Laughter breaks out all around me.

"There's snow-time like now!" John taunts.

"We have snow-coconuts today," a voice in the back pipes up.

"Without water, there's snow-showers for us!" Tari thinks he is funny.

It seems everyone has a snow idea.

"Maybe there's snow-devil, what do you think?" Tari's on a roll. His snub hurts. I feel simple-minded already, and I know he will not let me forget my mistake.

The pastor calls us to silence. His brows furrowed and his lips pressed together, he looks more earnest than I've ever seen him before. Slowly, he unfolds the newspaper he's brought in. I like the fact that his lessons are rooted in real life, like Bumbu Joshua's.

"Black Magic Implicated in the Death of Pregnant Woman on Tanna" scream large black letters on the front page of the newspaper.

"What do you know about Black Magic?" Father Ephraim asks the assembled students. I have heard of it, of course. Everyone has. It is part of our lives, and each of us is in awe and fear of it. Even on our island, we have had sudden illnesses or disappearances that could not be explained otherwise.

"My uncle saw a person morph into a flying squirrel," ventures a boy called Pascal, a senior. "If a magic man doesn't like another man, he can wait till the man goes fishing, then turn into a shark and eat him."

"I heard there are witch doctors on some of the islands," says Joachim, dread coloring his voice. "They can kill a man by shaking a handful of cobwebs at him."

"Some magicians can walk around without being seen by anybody. They boil a black cat, and then place one of the cat's bones in their mouth." I recognize Lois' voice. After his unkind remarks on the first day, I have never spoken to him again. Boiling a black cat seems like a powerful thing to do.

"A magic man can turn into a cat and climb in a window, and if you touch this cat, you will die." John is joining the discussion with fear in his voice. He's undoubtedly had a bad experience.

Everyone knows about magic. I know that we can't cut down a banyan tree without the clearance of a magic man. Bumbu Joshua told me it is because the spirits of the dead reside there. He loves to sit at the base of these majestic trees and commune with his ancestors. And I've seen Uncle Toka spit on the ground to make a wish come true.

"Now listen to me, all of you!" bellows the deep voice of Father Ephraim, full of authority. "How many times have you repeated that God is the only power? Do you really think a man can, through his will, make another die or change into a flying fox? People believe all sorts of things when they lack understanding, but there is always a rational explanation for those who know the facts. That's one of the reasons you are here at school, to find out facts and scientific explanations."

I would like to believe Father Ephraim, but I have too many unanswered questions flying around in my head. The whole assembly is quiet. I wonder how he can be so confident. *Is he right or Bumbu Joshua?* I think of the times we felt magic operate in our village, and all the times the spirits of our ancestors guided and protected us. I'm so confused. Whom should I believe?

"Storms are not Black Magic, and neither are volcanic eruptions. Death and illness have nothing to do with Black Magic. There is no Black Magic, only false beliefs." Father Ephraim's eyes scrutinize the reactions of his flock of wide-eyed students. Others must be looking dubious as well, for our pastor lets out a deep sigh. This subject matter is not yet sufficiently cleared up. We'll talk about it again and again, I'm sure.

He opens his Bible and bids us do the same. Together we read passages that reinforce what he has taught us. Kwevira, who is an excellent reader, spells out some familiar stories of healings that could have been called magic, too. How I love listening to her as she reads passages that Bumbu Joshua read to me under our navele tree.

The powerful diesel generator's hum fills the pauses. It provides electricity for the light that shines on this group of eager students each evening, just like a knowledgeable pastor shines the light on a dark topic like Black Magic.

==//==

Then, unavoidably, bedtime arrives. We scatter and make our way to our dorms. Between games and fights, discussions and preparations for the next day, we get ready for the night. My stomach growls. It's clamoring for something to calm it down. *I better put the books in order for tomorrow,* I think and reach for my satchel that lies limply on the cement floor under the bed. Just then, another cramp in my belly distracts me. I swallow hard, and I know I will not be able to fall asleep like this.

Again, my hand slides under the mattress, looking for the envelope. The small bundle of vatus will not cover such an expense every night, but I'm too hungry to care about this now. Without looking, I pull out a few bills and bury them deep in the pocket of my shorts. Cradling the precious currency in my right fist, I pretend to make a trip to the latrines.

There is no-one about. A few neon tubes flicker their blue light here and there. Out of the dark steps a big boy. I quicken my step. I'm not looking up, but Ho'okano steps right into my path. He hesitates for a moment. I walk around him and towards my goal, hand firmly on the crumpled vatus in my pocket.

Seconds later, two boys join him. I wonder briefly what they are up to.

"Hey, where are you going?" Luke is talking to me. I avert my eyes. *Just a hundred yards to the safety of the flickering neon lamp and the salesperson in the canteen.*

"We are talking to you, shrimp," Rodney says forcefully. My breath stops, and I can't answer. "Rude, too?"

"Or scared," Ho'okano observes. "He must be holding some vatus. We're hungry. How 'bout sharing?" His voice is low and menacing.

"No!" my whole being screams while my stomach is doing somersaults. I start to run, but Rodney catches me by the arm. In a split second, he's twisted it up behind me, making me scream in pain. I look for help, but because of the hibiscus bushes all around us, I see not a soul. I'm so close, but the pain that sears through my body paralyzes me. *My crackers are history.*

"Out with the money, wimp. We want to buy some goodies tonight." Ho'okano stands in front of me, stretching out his hand. I'm hooked in a hammerlock and can't move. The three laugh. I think Rodney is going to break my arm. The fist that grips the vatus is wet with sweat. A sharp nudge on my twisted arm makes the decision for me. I yank the right hand out of my pocket and throw the bills on the ground.

"Well done," Ho'okano mocks and bends down to pick up the sodden banknotes. Rodney releases my arm and with a kick in the back sends me sprawling. Even before I can get up, the thieves have vanished.

Silence surrounds me but for the wind that whispers in the bushes. The canteen's neon flickers coldly. I rub my shoulder. That was painful, but more painful than my shoulder is the pain in my heart. My stomach, desperate for some food, twists itself into a knot. Tears well up, and I sob uncontrollably as all the fear I felt a moment ago wracks my body. The shame in my defeat crushes me. *Bumbu Joshua, did you know about these things? What should I do?*

Chapter 10: Other Lands, Other Customs

My bruises are fading, but not the low grades in my English test.

"Abel, 68% is not enough. You have to work harder if you want to stay in my class." Mrs. Lawrence throws the test pages on my desk. "Uranui, 75% is nothing to boast about, either. John, 61%. Ask yourself whether school is the right choice for you. Tari, 82%. You could do better." Tari's smug grin burns a hole in my back. Of course, he doesn't have to deal with the trio of bullies. *Why not? Am I easier to scare? Did he send them… no, he could not be that mean.*

Mrs. Lawrence has no enemies breathing down her neck. She does not fear disappointing the one who loves her the most. Her life seems easy to me, yet she spreads fear on a daily basis. Only Kwevira and a handful of others remain in her favor. *I can't take it anymore, but what choice do I have?* I sigh. Then I vow to myself to catch up over the Easter holidays, which are just a few days ahead.

A knock turns all eyes to the classroom door. The moment our headmaster comes into view, the class falls silent. *What bad news is he going to hit us with?*

"The Mission in New Zealand is sponsoring a school trip for all boarders and will send buses to take you to Londot Village. Our school has been invited to watch the famous land divers we call Naghol," Mr. Wilson announces. "Of course, you will not miss the Combine church service in Lalwori on Easter Sunday and Monday." And with that, he leaves to spread the news to other classes.

Excitement rushes through the room. We don't know where Londot lies or what land diving is, and Mrs. Lawrence isn't going to tell us. We have to wait until geography class to get our answers.

"I need to study English to catch up," I ask Mr. Mangau. "Can I stay behind?"

"Everyone is going, without exception." And with that, my visions of extended hunting trips without fear of getting caught vanish.

==//==

The preacher at the Combine church service reminds us of the Good News of the Easter message: the death and resurrection of our Savior. The pastor's booming voice carries us back to the event two millennia ago. Both hands raised to heaven, he calls our attention to Jesus' triumphant entry into Jerusalem. We feel part of the adoring crowds of people who showed their devotion to the Messiah by laying their cloaks on the ground to welcome him.

"Jesus' entry into Jerusalem was very dramatic," the pastor prepares us. "He demanded, 'Untie the camel on which no one has sat,' and they loosed it and brought the camel to Jesus."

A camel? I can't help but snicker. Uranui elbows me on the right, chortling and practically falling from the bench. I glance left at John, who's squirming and biting his hand to avoid laughing out loud.

On Monday, the pastor reads about the resurrection of Jesus, and how believers would gain eternal life through their own resurrection.

"How does he know about eternity?" Uranui asks the group on our hike back to school.

"And who wants this kind of life to go on forever?" Kwevira raises her voice. "Kwevira, 99%. It is not good enough," she mimics Mrs. Lawrence's high-pitched voice, and we all laugh. I definitely would not want this kind of loneliness, fear and competition to go on forever.

Just as we arrive, sweaty and famished, back at the school, some beat-up buses pull up in the yard. We run to our dorms to pick up our backpacks, then to the kitchen to pick up some bananas and coconuts as sustenance for the trip. Many of us have never taken a bus ride in our lives. It's a tight squeeze through the folding doors and a scramble to find a seat, but I am amazed at how comfortable the seats are. The plastic-covered benches are far better than the planks on the truck that brought us to school more than two months ago.

Kwevira sits in the last row of the girls' section in the front of the bus. I sit in the first row of the boys' section right behind her. Her braids swing about as she talks to her neighbor. I try to hear what they are saying, but between the noise of the motor and the excited voices of the boys behind me, I can't. I'm sitting beside Uranui, my one true friend here, who's brought a string for cat's cradle and invites me to make the first move.

Our bus lurches out of the gate and jerks along a rough, rutted road. Heavy rainclouds darken the jungle path. Two hours later, I've eaten my banana, and already, my stomach growls again. Uranui fidgets. He clutches his stomach and moans. He needs to relieve himself, but the bus rolls on.

"If you need to make a stop, tell the driver," I suggest.

"He looks so mean," Uranui whines. "Can't you talk to him?" he pleads, his whole frame bunched into a ball. I put myself in his place for a moment, then I steel myself. *What's the worst thing that the driver can do to me?*

"OK, let me out," I say as I push past my friend. Holding on to anything I can grab, I step cautiously towards the front. The driver's gaze is fixed to the rutted road ahead. A bump makes me bang into his chair.

"Didn't I tell you to stay in your seats?" he growls without turning his head.

"We need to get out," I answer. Now I have to go, too.

"Sit down. We'll be there in half an hour."

I turn and glance at my fellow students. Some anxious faces confirm what I'm doing is right, and that we aren't the only ones who need to stop. Kwevira's head lolls about in sleep.

"If you don't stop, there will be an accident inside the bus." I stand firm, looking straight at him. *Where did that come from?* Even Kwevira opens her eyes in surprise. The bus slows down and comes to a stop. Several students take the opportunity to find a private tree or bush nearby. *I have a voice,* I smile to myself, *and the driver listened to it.*

The storm clouds menace, and we hurry back into the vehicle. Heavy drops of rain start to pelt the roof and windows of our bus. All of a sudden, the heavens open and our path is obscured by sheets of rain. The windshield wipers labor at top speed. All conversation stops. On the left, newly formed rivers seek a way to the ocean. Every time our driver fords one of these streams, the water splashes as high as our windows. On our right, angry gray ocean waves cover the beach with foam.

Fear creeps from my stomach into my throat. I wish I had been allowed to stay at school. I look around. Everyone's eyes are riveted to the road. We are not far now, maybe five miles, the driver tells us, but he's slowing the bus down. A look out the window shows us a newly formed river that may be too deep for the bus. Our driver seems to be debating what to do. After a short hesitation, he revs up the engine. We're going through. I grip the handle in front of me and hold on with all my strength.

The spray on both sides is higher than our bus. There is a jolt, and some students scream. Uranui's body slams into mine. The driver swears. The bus comes to a halt, tilted sharply to one side, in the middle of what is now a raging river. We are really, truly stuck. I pray our vehicle doesn't fall over. Kwevira whimpers.

With another torrent of swear words, the driver gets up from his seat. "Stay where you are and be quiet." His hoarse voice fills our refuge. "We'll have to wait until the water subsides. With a downpour like this, it may take a while." He sits down again and lights a cigarette. Water is seeping in through the driver's door. The windows are fogging up.

I tap Kwevira on the shoulder. Her nose is bleeding, and she is crying. I am shocked, but when I regain my wits, I call out for a handkerchief. Two hands shoot up. I take them both and go to the front.

"Can you hold these out the window to make them wet?" I demand. The driver obliges me. *Abel, you're a boss,* I congratulate myself. My flip-flops spray water with every step I take, as I pass one of the handkerchiefs to Kwevira.

"I want to go home," another girl wails. A bump on her forehead is swelling and turning blue. Others join her chorus.

"My knee is bleeding," Luke shouts from the back. Without his two beefy friends, he is just as scared as we all are. Holding on to every bench as I go, I pass the second handkerchief to him.

"I hurt my elbow." John is right beside me now. Even though I know I can't help him, I look at it. *There is nothing we can do but wait,* I think. Some cry, while others nurse their injuries. The rain drums onto the roof of our tilted shelter, and inside, moisture drips from the bus windows. We are alone out here. *What if the water drags us out into the ocean?*

Hours pass. Have the others already arrived? Did they turn around?

Within minutes, it becomes dark, but gradually, the rain lightens up.

"I think we have to walk the rest of the way," I suggest.

"No way!" John is the first to oppose my idea.

"It's dark, and we don't know where to go." Kwevira has a good point, but we are out of choices.

"My leg hurts," Luke's response flies through the blackness.

"Who has a better idea?" I shout. Nobody answers. I look at the driver, who knows how to get to Londot village. With another torrent of filthy oaths, he gets up and puts the keys into his pocket.

"Might as well," he mutters. "Stay together, and no whining even when it gets steep." He opens the front door, and I'm the first to clamber up to it. Our tilt means I have to jump to get to the ground. I sit on the ledge and ease down into the river with a splash. The water rushes up to my knees.

With the help of our driver, the bus is soon evacuated. Then our little group stands in the rain, facing him, waiting to find out where to go.

He takes off at high speed. The night is pitch-black, as neither moon nor stars shine through the layer of clouds. A night bird screeches. I hold Kwevira's arm, and together we navigate roots and rocks, mud and uprooted bushes on the road. The way gets steeper as we turn inland. Occasionally, there is a shout of distress from one, or some encouragement from another, but all together we stay behind our guide as best we can.

Wet, hungry, tired and hurt, we are a bedraggled lot as we arrive in the village of Londot. Villagers, teachers and students are all assembled around a roaring fire. As soon as they see the first of us, they come running. I can't help but smile at Kwevira. *We did it!*

Mr. Mangau thanks the driver, shaking his hand. His face beams with a huge and happy smile. He is so relieved, he's almost dancing from one student to the other as he's welcoming us.

Chief Luke Waga says a few words in the Sa language,

which our teacher translates into Bislama. Then we finally get to feast on yams cooked in coconut milk and boiled fish, and there is plenty of it. We forget all etiquette and descend upon the food like locusts. Now I'm glad I came to Londot. English can wait.

It turns out that only a few of the adults speak Bislama here, and none of them a word of English. We would not be able to communicate at all were it not for gestures and facial expressions. I try to understand the best I can as our hosts and teachers talk about the events of the next day.

As we sit together, I have a question burning on my lips. "Why do your men risk their lives by jumping to the earth from such a high tower built of branches?"

Rather than be angry for questioning their customs, one of the elders tells us the story of the beginning of the event they call Gol:

"Long ago, a young and cruel man named Tamalie lived on the island of Pentecost. When he had chosen a young woman to be his wife, she vehemently refused. She tried to run away, but Tamalie had made up his mind, and he followed her into the jungle. He saw in the distance that his chosen wife climbed to the top of a huge banyan tree. Tamalie climbed the same tree, and branch by branch he was catching up with her.

"He was wondering how high she would go, but eventually, she stopped. Tamalie kept climbing and climbing, getting closer to her. Just as he was close enough to grab her, she threw herself into the void. Tamalie followed her down but killed himself upon landing. The young woman, on the other hand, got up unscathed. She had tied vines onto her feet that she had attached to a strong branch.

Ever since that time, this custom has been performed by men, so they would not be tricked again, and also to show how courageous they are. That, in turn, persuades the spirits to give us a good yam harvest."

"It takes much knowledge to collect timber and vines to build a tower that is almost 100 feet high," our teacher translates. "Each platform must be built exactly according to the height and weight of the diver and must break at push-off. The diver's shoulder must brush against the ground." His words conjure up scary scenarios in my mind. What if a vine stretches so much that a diver's head slams into the ground, breaking his neck?

"This year, Ernest is the youngest diver. He is only eight. He was circumcised last year." I can't believe the words our teacher is relaying to us. "He will jump in the presence of his elders to prove that he is ready to leave his childhood behind. His platform is the lowest, and he will be up first. Ernest's father is the last diver. He will jump from the highest platform. This act of bravery will ensure his status as chief of the village."

I am fascinated by the different ways that village chiefs are created. How much courage it must take to jump from such a height. I'm not sure I'd be brave enough to do it, and I'm glad such a ritual is not required in our tribe. I wonder if this kind of bravery is also a sign of courage in other ways, like challenging a bully, facing up to Black Magic or confronting an invader.

"When will the ceremony start?" Joachim asks the teacher.

Just then, in the distance, we see a crowd building up, approaching our group with torches. In the orange light, we can see about twenty men, with panicked women dashing around them.

Chief Luke Waga gets up and greets the man we learn is Chief Bule from Wali, a village down by the ocean. My heart beats wildly. It looks like they've come to start a war.

I look around. Kwevira and her friends are watching from the opposite side of the U-shaped seating arrangements. I love it when she is in my sight even when we are in a crowd. Kwevira has made herself small, hiding between the girls sitting around her as they hug each other.

I wish I could protect her in some way. Maybe, if things get bad, we could run away to a safe place in the village. I wonder what Bumbu Joshua would do in such a situation.

The men assemble in a sudden nakamal, and kava is served by the boys of Londot village. The atmosphere is tense, and we hardly dare to breathe. For a moment, flashes of the confrontation between Chief Mui and Bumbu Joshua come to mind, and I remember how their arguments swayed the audience.

"Justice often is fluid, my boy," Bumbu Joshua had said to me that day. "You can twist and stretch and turn a fact, and people will react, depending on your gift of persuasion. The more eloquent you are, the more successfully you will get your point across. Sometimes only the spirits know what the truth is."

My bottom hurts, and I fidget on the hard log. A chicken walks along the edge of the nasara, as if to draw away the attention from what's happening. I take my chance and duck behind the backs of the onlookers. Stealthily, and without making a noise, I move towards the log the girls are sitting on. I tap Kwevira's arm.

"What's happening here?" she whispers.

"I don't know what's going on, but if you are scared, we can run to one of the huts together," I whisper back, shakily.

"Are you crazy?" She swats at me as you would a fly. I'm disappointed, but running by myself would make me look like a coward. Bending low, I carefully hide behind the backs of the bewildered students and regain my seat without being noticed. The men of both tribes are standing around the fire drinking kava.

Chief Bule's behavior strikes me as terribly impolite. He is not at all concerned that he is interrupting an important event. His angry words ring out over the nasara. He gesticulates wildly, but there is no guessing what his grievance might be.

"Stray bullocks have escaped and utterly destroyed the gardens of the people in Wali," Mr. Mangau relates to those who sit near him. Fierce shouts and fearsome gestures rise in support from the men behind Chief Bule. "The garden of an Elder was demolished, and the crops were laid to waste," our teacher says.

We are spellbound. The whole situation is so tense I barely dare to breathe. Nobody is uttering a word. Naturally, I feel much closer to our host than to the intruding neighbors. I glance over at Mr. Mangau. His attention, too, is tightly focused on the doings in the nasara. Even the coconut palms and the giant banyan trees are leaning in to listen.

Suddenly, Joachim pokes me hard in the ribs. It catches me off guard, and with a short cry, I fall backward from my perch onto the dusty ground.

As I clumsily try to get back up onto my seat on the log, Chief Waga's eyes search the assembly for the disruption. "If you have something to say, do it now," Mr. Mangau translates the chief's words. Every eye now turns towards me, and I wish the earth would swallow me whole.

I'm on the spot. Kwevira is looking straight at me. *With a few clever words, I might impress her,* I think, and I stand up. "Chief Bule, Chief Waga, we have heard each of you state your side of the argument." I look at Mr. Mangau, as he translates my message into Bislama for the sparring chiefs. My voice is clear, and the admiring look on Kwevira's face gives me wings.

I try to be impartial, even though I hate to see our hosts upset over this matter. "It is evident that hard proof is necessary to find what kind of penalty you can force upon this clan." Mr. Mangau translates my words, directing them at Chief Bule,

I notice Chief Bule nodding as he stares at me. Other men hold their heads still but gaze at each other. The wind is hushed, and the cicadas suspend their song. Even the moon now stares down at us. I wish it would calm the giddy, explosive mood.

Chief Bule steps towards the center. His voice seems much calmer now, his thoughts more focused than before. He raises both hands. "First of all, we thank the esteemed visitor for his words." His eyes turn in the direction where Joachim and I are clustered. My heart pounds. Proudly, I lift my head when Mr. Mangau relays the message. "Nonetheless, we, the people of Wali, must put a monetary value on the damage done to our property."

Apart from the fire-spewing cinders, total silence envelops us.

"One more thing." Chief Bule now turns in the direction of Mr. Mangau. "I believe school teaches students respect and obedience according to the Bible, just like our children learn it from the elders here in Wali and Londot." He gives Mr. Mangau time to translate. My heart stops for a moment. This is not good.

Chief Bule emphasizes his words by lifting both hands even higher in the sky. "Respect works both ways, especially if you are a visitor to a foreign community. Does your school not teach its students not to interfere in other people's business?" These words hit me as hard as a stone from a slingshot. Worse, I am not the only target – my teacher is as well. Moreover, I have exposed the whole school.

What I said may have made sense in my own boastful mind, but 'once a word is said, it can never be made unsaid.' Way too late, I think of our religious study teacher telling us to think before we speak. *Fool, fool, fool!* I reprimand myself.

Chief Waga's eyes burn holes into me for an instant, then he turns away from me and my teacher. "Chief Bule, you can assure yourself that all my bullocks are perfectly fenced in. Their pasture is good, and they don't need to break out and find pasture in your gardens. Besides, there are many other chiefs keeping cattle. You still have not given us any evidence that this calamity is our fault." Mr. Mangau keeps us informed about the men's discussion.

Chief Waga's remarks are like gunpowder to Chief Bule's shotgun. He raises his voice even before Chief Waga can sit down. "We, the people of Wali, have decided to value the damage at 20,000 vatus, payable immediately. You may come and see the damage any time you want. Moreover, we demand that payment be made without delay and before this ceremony resumes."

Chief Luke Waga listens to the charges, and then, while the heckling visitors are being served another shell of island kava, he apologizes to them. He doesn't even protest the high fine. *What is he thinking?* All the people of Londot are holding their breaths.

Now Chief Luke Waga huddles with his son and some of his men. After a short while, he makes an announcement. "People from Wali, Chief Bule, we apologize and will be even more vigilant in the future. As you well know, we are not in possession of 20,000 vatus. Will you accept a bullock as compensation?"

"Sometimes it's better to avoid an argument by giving in early," I remember Bumbu Joshua saying, and sure enough, Chief Waga's words send the whole nakamal into cheers and clapping of approval. To my surprise, Chief Bule gets up and thanks the Chief of Londot. Then he even apologizes to the teachers and students of Ranwadi High for the delay and disruption.

What just happened? How was this war averted? Chief Waga had listened deeply and agreed that his adversary had a point. Then he made amends as quickly as possible. *Bumbu Joshua would have posed more questions. He would have negotiated more, trying to lessen the penalty.* Nevertheless, Bumbu Joshua also said, "Abel, you do not always have to win an argument. The Spirits always know who is right." I make a note about this new knowledge for the future.

A short prayer by the two parties is followed by handshakes. Chief Waga's wisdom is praised. Burning torches held high, the intruding party retires, and makes its way back to Wali. Chief Waga approaches the fireside again. "Apologies to our visitors and those who dare the dive tomorrow. Naghol will proceed in the early morning, as planned."

Turning to Mr. Mangau, and giving pause after each sentence for the translation, he explains, "Before dawn, all the divers will have a ritual wash. Then they put coconut oil over their bodies and paint it according to their family tradition. By their curved boar tusks around their necks, you can tell which social rank they have achieved."

"Can women also show their courage this way?" one of the

girls asks.

"No, no! The women dance and sing to make the men more courageous. But they have to stay away from the structure, because Tamalie's spirit may seek revenge and kill one of the young divers. The women watch, though, you can be sure!"

By now the fire has burnt itself out. I am exhausted. The men retire to the men's sleeping house. It is dark except for a faint shimmer of the moon behind the clouds, and we can barely see the rocks and bushes on our path.

"Ouch, shoot, shoot, shoot!" Tari is shouting in a muffled voice. *Serves him right,* is my first thought, but as I come near, I see he's on the ground, hugging his knee. "This stupid hole came out of nowhere, and I almost broke my leg!" he wails.

Just get up and move, I want to say, but instead, I bend down and ask, "Is there anything I can do?"

Tari looks at me in surprise. I put my hand on his knee, just as Kwevira did on my wrists when I suffered on the boat. "Try to put weight on it," I suggest. "I'll help you get to the sleeping house." He furrows his brows but then looks me in the eyes and grabs my outstretched hand. He manages to get upright, and together, we make it to the sleeping house. Each one of us chooses a spot on the ground. I bundle up my knapsack as a pillow and soon fall asleep.

==//==

The call of a fan-tailed cuckoo wakes me, like it often did in my own village. For a moment I think I am home with Bumbu Joshua. But no, the familiar voices of my classmates fill the room.

I have managed to think of home without the usual firebolt in my stomach, I think, and I smile. I am impatient to see and learn and experience how the people of Londot live and celebrate life.

As each one of us wakes up, we gather outside in the common area. A long plank on the ground is covered with banana leaves piled high with mango, banana and yams baked in the earth-oven overnight. I'm so excited about this feast we share with our hosts. Sadly, we cannot share many words. Our teacher does it for us and keeps us informed about the day's happenings. His eyes rest on me for a long while. "We have to talk."

Then we join the villagers who make their way to the mountain. It is a short walk to the foot of the tower. The sun already burns down on us, making us sweat. Amid excited shouts and impatient pushing, I walk in silence. Kwevira is walking with the other girls close to the teacher, who is leading our group. She must have felt my stare, because she turns back towards me and sends me a smile, making me feel special again.

Logs have been put in neat rows for spectators to sit on. From here, we have a good view of the tower, which was built midway up the hill. Soon everyone is seated. In the distance, the beat of tam-tams fills the air. At the top of the hill, a group of men of all ages is chanting and dancing. Women dressed in their grass skirts stand at a certain distance, with some of them holding young children by the hand or carrying babies.

The chanting and dancing intensify. We look up. There is Ernest, approaching the tower without looking around. He cautiously climbs up to the first platform, about ten feet up.

Two elders fasten vines around his ankles. Ernest looks towards heaven and makes the sign of the cross on his forehead and his chest. Then he folds his arms over his chest, lets out a loud cry, and throws himself in the air. The platform snaps with a crack. A sharp intake of breath from all the spectators fills the air. Kwevira is pressing both her hands to her eyes, peeking at the event through her fingers.

Ernest's left shoulder skims the freshly raked ground. For an instant, he hangs upside down. I fear Ernest has jumped to his death. His older brother rushes towards him and hugs him tightly. Two elders untie the vines, and the young hero stands up. His eyes go to the top of the hill, where his mother stands, waving a small green toy. At this moment she throws it behind her.

"He has left boyhood behind. He is now an adult," our teacher remarks.

"I'd jump from the second platform for you," I whisper to Kwevira. Something makes me want to get her attention. I want to let her know I can be brave, too.

"I'd love to see you do that!" answers Tari, who heard my words. "I would jump from the third platform myself!" *No, you wouldn't, you braggart,* I think, and am surprised at how annoyed I am. Kwevira takes her hands off her face and rewards me with a tiny smile. How pretty her eyes look. Heat spreads like a rash from my stomach to my head.

Six other men dare the dive. As the divers climb higher and higher, the anxiety in our group grows. Next, and last, is Ernest's father. I can already see him climbing to the highest platform of the scaffold. The sun comes out behind a cloud for a moment, making his body gleam. After the vines are attached to his ankles, he stands there.

Drumming fills the air. I hold my breath. Nobody speaks a word, while all eyes are riveted to the scaffold.

"This is for you, Maeva!" he calls out to his wife. He shouts more words we do not understand. "I love this land and all the people in my tribe!" Our teacher translates the mighty voice that seems to come right out of heaven. "May the harvest be plentiful this year and feed us and give us round bellies!"

With this, he crosses his hands over his chest and hurls his gleaming body off the highest platform. As he pushes off, it fractures with a loud crack and sends the jumper into the void.

If one of the vines breaks, he is dead, I think to myself, hardly daring to watch as his body gets whipped back at the end of his fall. Two men rush towards Ernest's father and embrace him tightly, while others untie the vines. Then, the hero throws up his hands in triumph. Screams and cheers fill the air, and everyone jumps to their feet as he climbs back up the hill to rejoin the other men. Everyone in our group talks at once.

"Could you do that?" our teacher asks nobody in particular. His voice is full of admiration. I do not repeat my offer to jump.

For my part, I fervently hope we will not be invited to prove our bravery. My offer to jump from the second platform was more like a verbal gift to Kwevira. I'm relieved that there were no accidents, and I flop back onto my seat and let my eyes scan the heavens. The bright sun makes me squint. The air is full of excited shouts.

Soon we all go back to the village, where we are spending the rest of the day with our new friends. Among the boys, all talk revolves around diving and other acts of bravery. The girls are helping with food preparation. *No language skills needed here*, I think and wish I could in some way contribute.

Early the next morning, it is time to bid our hosts goodbye. The buses are waiting for us outside the village to take us back to Ranwadi for two very busy months of preparation for the end-of-semester exams. The competition to keep a good class rank will be fierce. This makes me as nervous as thinking about jumping from a platform with only a liana keeping me alive.

Mr. Mangau takes me aside before I can follow Uranui onto the bus. "You will report to the headmaster as soon as we arrive, young man. You have some impulsive behavior to explain."

And with that weight around my neck, I sit beside Uranui, not speaking a word for the whole duration of the trip. *Don't go so fast*, I silently implore the driver.

84

Chapter 11: School Life

"You have embarrassed the whole school in front of the people of Londot and Wali," Mr. Wilson thunders. I had feebly knocked on his door and entered when told to do so. Sitting in the gray folding chair before him, I am barely able to breathe. Given a choice, I'd climb the tower in Londot right now and wait for the liana to be tied to my foot.

He removes his glasses and gets up from behind the enormous desk, step by step closing the gap between us. The blue veins on his neck bulge. The button on his jacket strains in rhythm with every sentence he hurls in my direction. Even the ring of white curls that remind me of Bumbu Joshua manages to look menacing.

"Who asked you for your opinion, Abel Nako?" I sink ever deeper into myself. Soon there will be nothing left, except maybe my hair. A smile creeps onto my lips at the thought of a bushel of hair lying on the chair where I had been.

"You find that funny, Abel? Have you no respect for authority?" Why is he shouting so loud when I'm sitting at arm's length from him? My stomach is tying itself into a knot, and now I just want to cry.

"You should be expelled from this school," Mr. Wilson practically shouts into my ear. "Where is your bravery now? Have you nothing to say for yourself?"

His eyes are piercing mine. I slide off the chair and stand before the man.

"I – I – I um—" Where is my voice? I clear my throat and start again. "I apologize for what I did," I say. "I thought Chief Waga had asked me. My – my grandfather often took me to the nakamal. And back home he would ask what I thought. I never meant to – to—"

What bad thing did I actually do?

"Go now and put your name on the detention list for next Saturday. I will talk with your teachers and will let you know tomorrow what we will do with you. You are dismissed." Mr. Wilson opens the door and ushers me out.

Slowly, I amble through the hallway, joining my class when it is almost finished. Every eye turns to me, and I blush deep red as I slide back into my seat beside Uranui. Mr. Mangau writes our homework onto the blackboard and leaves after the bell rings. The class buzzes like a nest of hornets.

"How was it?" Kwevira's voice is full of concern.

"Bunbun Karong, the bony fish, talked to the big sharks, and they didn't like it," Joachim taunts, provoking laughter all around.

"I may be expelled," I offer quietly, hoping to appease the taunting with this shocker of bad news. And indeed, the crowd around me falls silent.

"If they send you home, I go with you." Bless Kwevira for sticking up for me. "You did nothing but answer because you thought you were asked. On top of that, what you said made good sense." Her words are like honey in my parched throat. I wonder if she really would come with me.

At the sound of the bell, Mrs. Lawrence steps into our class room. She practically throws a pile of notebooks on her desk. Catching one before it slides to the floor, she says, "You know that only the top students get a 'very good.' What most of you wrote was rubbish."

Then she proceeds to hand out our essays one by one, critiquing each student's efforts verbally. She makes sure to point out every single mistake so others can make fun of it. What humiliation! Never could I imagine someone in our village school shaming a student this way. Does Mrs. Lawrence think put-downs and the fear of failing will make us work harder?

In our class, everyone knows who received the lowest score, the highest, and who hovers around the middle. The status of a pupil is expressed in a percentile, and that number defines each of us.

My score not only defines me and my efforts but apparently also my intelligence. It affects the way a teacher or a classmate judges me, and it definitely affects how I judge myself. If I drop some percentile, I feel crushed for the whole week. I start to see everyone in my class, even my friends, as competitors. And what else is a competitor than an enemy?

My grade could have been worse, I think, but I vow to work harder. Then I remember this morning's visit with Mr. Wilson. An arrow shoots through my stomach. *Heck, if I get expelled, what's the use? Bumbu Joshua, I'm so sorry!* I spend recess alone, wallowing in my shame.

The last class of the day is geography. By now I don't see the point of even attending classes anymore. Mr. Mangau enters, and right behind him, Mr. Wilson. *Oh, no, now comes the end,* I think and swallow hard to stop my stomach from turning itself inside out. *I will not cry in front of everyone here.* Silence falls over the class. Nobody stirs.

"You all know Abel's behavior was not appropriate," begins Mr. Wilson. "But it has come to my attention that he acted because of a misunderstanding. It also came to my attention that he handled the situation well when the bus stalled. He looked after his classmates and supported those who got hurt. Is that so?" Mr. Wilson looks into the classroom, and a few murmurs rise.

"Abel Nako, for this time you are exempt from detention." And with that, Mr. Wilson turns to leave. A weight falls from my shoulders.

"Thank you. And I will do my best from here on." I can't help myself. Kwevira's smile makes me want to jump up and down and sing at the top of my voice. Instead, I force myself to sit down. Yet I can't subdue the big grin on my face.

==//==

From now until the end of June, we are all caught in a frenzy of studies, with the only aim of getting good grades before going home for the three week holiday in July.

Kwevira spends most of her lunch breaks and evenings in the library, studying for the English exam. Today she is writing an essay, but she's willing, as always, to help me with a tricky homework assignment. Dorica, another girl in our class, is sitting beside her, also asking questions from time to time.

I hear a commotion outside. Kwevira is writing furiously. She hears nothing, but I walk to the window to see what's going on.

"It looks like Judith and Francie have caught a chicken for their home economics exam," I whisper.

Kwevira looks up, a bit annoyed, but she's intrigued by all the clucking and shouting outdoors. She pushes back her chair and momentarily abandons her notebooks.

In the sunlight outside, the two girls are breathless. The body of the scrawny fowl twitches and strains against Judith's blue t-shirt, its glossy brown feathers glinting in the sunlight. Francie's arms almost squash the poor creature for fear that it might escape. Now Judith and Francie are demonstrating how they have been taught to execute the bird. Kwevira covers her eyes with both hands. Tentatively, she lifts one finger. The chicken will be baked in the school oven the following day, as part of the exam.

"We will have to do this next year," I say confidently, thinking back to the bird I shot on my first hunting excursion so long ago. Hungry as I was, I savored it the very next day. I have wrung many a bird's neck since then, roasted it and often shared my quarry with her. I yank my shoulders back and straighten my posture as a smile steals across my face.

Kwevira is silent. *Girls will never be good hunters,* I think. She hates killing any animal, even if her life depended on it. She turns around and goes back to the library to study until the dinner bell rings.

When it does, we hurry to the dining hall. It is dark by now, and Kwevira puts her arm around Dorica, while I walk by myself. Loneliness pokes her cold fingers right into my heart. I wish I were Dorica.

The same loneliness still grips me after the dinner of thin potato soup. I wash my utensils and decline an invitation to play soccer. I'm not in the mood to play ball or even talk to anybody. I slowly make my way to the dorm, wondering if I should venture to the canteen later for some crackers.

Muffled voices disturb my contemplations and make me look up. The bushes move in a peculiar way. Nervously, under cover of darkness and hibiscus bushes, I approach the scene, but not without picking up half a coconut shell as a potential weapon.

With a jolt to my stomach, I realize that a well-known trio of bullies has found another victim. I can practically feel their blows on my own body. *What to do? What to do?* I silently shout heavenwards. Doing nothing would be the same as being a participant. *But fighting three? After the kind of defeat I suffered at their hands?*

I can't just sit here! Stepping out of my cover, I recognize Uranui being held down by Luke and Ho'okano. At the same moment, a powerful blow in the face makes me see stars. I lose my balance. All of a sudden, red hot anger wells up in me, and I sink my teeth into Rodney's hand before it can disappear. I taste blood. Yuck! I spit it in Rodney's face in disgust, then I scream at the top of my lungs.

I grab Rodney's collar and drag it down with all the force I can muster. Then I thrash his head with the coconut shell. *They're going to kill us,* I think, as a kick in my ribs takes my breath away. I crash my weapon into the nearest face with all the strength I've got. Then I let out another scream as long as my breath allows. My voice is hoarse but still loud.

The three bullies look at each other, dumbfounded. Steps approach in a hurry, the beam of a flashlight pierces the darkness. Within a second, the three flee the scene. Uranui gets up and wipes blood from his nose while I wipe my chin. Mr. Mangau appears and lifts his torch into my face, then my friend's.

Another detention, I think, and my heart sinks. My face burns so bad, it must be glowing; and my rib hurts with every breath I take. But I know that one bully will have a headache and another a bandaged hand tomorrow. Then it dawns on me what I did, and I smile broadly. *Meek Abel kicks the brutes*. I didn't know I had it in me. Neither did they.

"He helped me," Uranui whispers, suppressing sobs. Mr. Mangau looks at us for a moment. He understands. There will be no detention for us. On Saturday we will get to watch three sixth-graders hack at the jungle grass with their machetes, while the sun mercilessly blazes down on them.

Chapter 12: Returning Home

All the students who leave the island during school vacation stand at the pier of Waterfall on this Anniversary of Independence Day. Tari, Kwevira and I are returning home, and I am excited to leave. I wish I could have bought some gifts from the canteen to bring back to my brothers, but alas, the money ran out a couple of weeks ago.

We watch while crates of kava root, coffee, coconut, copra and taro are loaded and secured on the inter-insular cargo boat. I hope the weather stays favorable during the long ride home. I feel like an adult now – much more so than right after my initiation ceremony. For one, I'm not afraid to make this voyage, and I can't wait to see my family again.

I have grown, which is something I can't say about my favorite t-shirt. My frequent hunting expeditions have not only made my stomach happier but also my mind clearer. Even getting caught every so often was not as dreadful as I had imagined. Some Saturday detentions could not be avoided, and the physical work made me tougher.

My new knowledge gives me courage. I have so many things to share and discuss with Bumbu Joshua. I have witnessed cultures and languages neither he nor I had ever heard of. Respect and awe rise in my heart for the different ways people live and honor their beliefs.

I've discovered how brave a man can be, and even found some of that bravery in myself. I smile as I think of the bullies that used to make my school life miserable. They've been avoiding me ever since I stepped in to help my friend. I know now that bullies are not necessarily courageous, and victims are not always meek.

Most of all, I am armed with a renewed and reinforced knowledge of the power of our Creator. The text of the Good News Gospel is more and more becoming the basis of my actions and thoughts.

Three long blasts of the ship's horn tell us it's time to board. Soon we settle between the crates, stacks and bags. Everyone's thoughts are already at their destination. The journey is long and uncomfortable but uneventful. The sea is calm, the scorching sun dimmed by a thin layer of cloud. Small groups of friends chatter and play games, and I even manage a short nap. To think a few short months ago, I was sick during this whole passage. It seems so much easier now.

Upon arrival at our village's pier, Tari, Kwevira and I find an unusually quiet welcome. There is no singing and dancing on the beach as our cargo ship pulls into port.

As soon as the ropes are secured, all three of us jump onto the pier. Only Molrongo is standing there, and I am disappointed that Bumbu Joshua or Uncle Toka didn't come to welcome me home. The only other people on the pier are Kwevira's mother and one of Tari's uncles. They greet their family members and soon duck away to hurry to their homes, disappearing without the usual happy greetings and welcomes.

"Let's rush home," Molrongo says. "It's not safe out here."

I am confused but ask no questions. The pier empties quickly. Only the ship's crew is working as usual.

"Strange things are happening," Molrongo tells me as we are half running to get home. "We have put special stones around most of the houses in our village for spiritual protection." Molrongo is a bit out of breath as he leads me to my dad's hut, where the whole family is gathered. I look for Bumbu Joshua. Uncle Toka greets me with a hug, and after him, every member of my family.

"Bumbu Joshua is not well," Uncle Toka says as if reading my thoughts. My heart beats wildly. *I need to see him.* "I think they used sorcery to hurt him. He spoke out against the strangers staying in our territory."

"What strangers?" I look at my uncle, who is more nervous than I've ever seen him. He's not looking me in the eye but keeps on talking.

"They're using Black Magic to hurt us," Uncle Toka explains, and I sense real fear in his voice. "A week ago," he continues in a hushed voice, "visitors from a tribe on the island of Malekula made an appearance."

"Why? Are they visiting relatives?" I ask.

"They have no relatives here. They were trying to settle on our island."

I don't understand why anyone would leave their tribe and settle among people they don't know.

"They want to start a business with sailboats on our shore."

"With their sailboats?" I ask. I can't imagine what use sailboats are to them, or to us. Every fisherman in our village has a boat already, and hunters have no reason to venture out into the ocean.

"They are hoping to attract a steady flow of tourists, people from other countries all over the world, to discover our way of life and the natural beauty of our island."

"To do what?" I am clearly not understanding something.

"They want to be ready to make money off of them," Uncle Toka spells it out for me. "They want to entice people from far-off lands to spend time on our island and go out in sailboats while they are here. They have already started to build their huts at the outskirts of our village.

"But nobody wants a constant flow of tourists to disturb our ways of life. Nobody wants groups of people from other countries to come through our village and poke their noses into our huts," Uncle Toka continues. "Maybe, once in a while, it is all right for a special occasion, but not on a regular basis."

"Then bad things started to happen," Molrongo adds. "Lokin stopped barking. He vanished three days ago."

"The pier, where the cargo ships fasten their ropes to unload their goods, was damaged." Uncle Toka looks out the window. "Also, the huge mango tree shading our nasara dropped all its fruit before it was ripe. But the worst thing is, Bumbu Joshua left for the mountain hut several days ago and has not come back. He made it clear that he wanted nobody to go with him. Everyone is worried."

Uncle Toka is not looking at me. He is staring out the window as if he was expecting someone to come. All my brothers and sisters, Mama Lovatu and Bumbu Janet sit around on the floor of the hut, saying nothing.

"Me harem se," 'me hear them say' in Bislama, "they want to open a fishing and sailing port for tourists." Uncle Toka is speaking to no one in particular. "This could mean employment for money..." His voice trails off.

"I'm going out to see Bumbu Joshua!" I exclaim. I can't stand to stay in this fearful environment a moment longer. I learned in school that sorcery cannot harm people, so certainly Bumbu Joshua must be alright. *But is that still true on Ambae?* For as long as I can remember, sorcery has been the explanation for so many mishaps, diseases and unfortunate events.

Father Ephraim had called these events 'things we can't explain'. We often discussed the matter with our pastor, who found not a single example in the New Testament, where people had to deal with such sorcery. Miracles, yes, but not sorcery.

"There is no Black Magic, only false beliefs," our pastor's words come back to me. Could there be another explanation for what is happening in my village?

Nobody tries to stop me when I leave the hut. The village is empty, save for some pigs tethered to their poles and waiting to be fed. Could Bumbu Joshua have separated himself from his family to spend his last days alone? Could he have decided to pass into the next life without anybody around? I run to our hut halfway up the trail to the mountain garden.

"Bumbu Joshua!" No answer. I don't understand. "Bumbu Joshua, it's me, Abel!" I circle the hut, shouting Bumbu's name. I listen. A tiny whine tells me that Lokin, faithful dog that he is, must be nearby. I push the door open and let my eyes adjust to the darkness inside.

There is a small figure curled up on the cot, buried under a mountain of covers. And there is a wet nose that touches my knee as I bend down to touch Bumbu Joshua. Lokin wriggles out from under the covers and goes crazy. His excitement at seeing me knows no bounds, and he yelps and jumps to lick my face. I am relieved to find our faithful dog here; it means Bumbu Joshua has not been completely alone all these days. I try to calm Lokin by petting him and hugging his quivering body, but the commotion wakes Bumbu Joshua. When he sees me, his lips form a smile.

"Abel!" Bumbu Joshua welcomes me. His mouth is dry, and he forces the words out. "Bring me a drink, my boy." His words are almost inaudible. Bumbu Joshua tries to get up. It takes all my strength to assist him, but I manage to hold him upright. He sits back on the cot while he drinks from the coconut I offer him.

"I've been poorly, my boy; it's the heart, I think." Bumbu Joshua looks ancient. I want to tell him everything I have experienced since I left him in February, but I realize this is not the moment to do so.

"Are the strangers still in the village?" he asks. I am hurt that this issue interests him more than I do.

"Yes, they are. You need to call a meeting at the nakamal."

Chapter 13: Tradition Meets Change

I make many trips from our mountain hut to the village. Three times a day, I carry up food for Bumbu Joshua. I massage his knees, and I walk a few steps with him as often as he has the energy. As we talk about the matter with the strangers, I begin to understand the situation better.

"Abel, we don't want our way of life to be lost," Bumbu Joshua says.

"I know what you mean," I answer and think about the pressures, the competition and the hunger in our school on Pentecost.

"Of course, there are benefits to having roads and shops," Bumbu Joshua looks far away. "But not all the changes are good ones. Remember Taman, who lives halfway up the hill near the nasara?" I do and can't help but feel a bit sorry for the man, whose son left four years ago to go to work on the island of Espirito Santo. He has not heard from his son since.

"These strangers are his son's friends," Bumbu Joshua continues. "They have a fishing and sailing business in Luganville. And they want to set up their business near our village."

"Paul came back from living in town because he did not want to deal with the stress of making money to survive," I say. As it is now, we have all we need. We never go hungry, and money is not required for day-to-day life. Parents only start to worry about money once they have children whom they want to send away to boarding school for higher education. I try to imagine life with everyone having to worry about earning money for survival.

"And here is another point, Abel." I lean towards Bumbu Joshua to hear his voice. "I have not heard many stories about money making people happy. Quite the contrary, in fact."

==//==

A couple of days later, Bumbu Joshua seems strong enough to make his way to the nakamal. A meeting with the strangers is arranged for the late afternoon. After a light meal and a long rest, we make our way to the men's meeting house. Bumbu's right hand reaches for my arm to steady himself. Walking at a snail's pace, he picks every one of his steps carefully.

"We're almost there, Bumbu," I encourage him, just as his leg gives way and he threatens to sink to the ground. I quickly support his frail body with both arms and manage to keep him upright.

"Stop here for a moment," Bumbu Joshua's voice is not much more than a sigh. He needs to catch his breath. I stop, still supporting him with both arms, and listen to the chorus of animal life all around us. Sweat pearls on my forehead. How many more meetings will Bumbu Joshua be able to hold?

We arrive at the nasara ahead of everyone else. Together we enter the hallowed place, and I help Bumbu Joshua get comfortable on his log. I wipe my forehead.

We are alone. "Bumbu Joshua, I wonder if they have considered the port of Waterfall for their business. It's beautiful there! And they'd already have a perfect dock and even roads to nearby villages."

"Even there they couldn't just set up a business," Bumbu replies thoughtfully. "They'd have to consult with the people living nearby. That won't be easy." I nod. It seems setting up a business is never easy, but starting out with angry neighbors must make it even harder.

"Why don't those who want to make money do so on other islands? There are more than 80 to choose from. Why on Ambae?" I ask.

"There are fewer rules here, and land is still cheap in comparison, but they need to find someone willing to sell it to them." I had not considered any of that before.

Most of the men of our village arrive at the same time and arrange themselves in a circle. The three visitors are seated together; they are young men from a neighboring island with a language of their own. Frank is a big fellow with curly hair down to his shoulders. He seems to be the one in charge. To his left sits a shorter man called Lucian. His face is framed in carefree dreadlocks, and he flashes a mouth full of perfect teeth whenever he smiles. And to his right, a somber-looking man they call Alphonse is stroking a full beard that covers much of his face.

Even though they don't speak our language, they know the nakamal is a place of peace and respect where no angry words are ever exchanged, and no one can be touched.

"Speak Bislama, so we can all understand," Bumbu Joshua counsels them. He tells everyone that these three men are friends of Taman's son, Patrick. I wonder where Patrick ended up and what he is doing.

Bumbu Joshua lights his pipe and nods his head to signal that the meeting may begin. Pastor Vocor Benadeth starts the tok-tok with a prayer. Then everyone gets a turn to explain his position and opinion. The young men tell the villagers how much money they could make.

"You could send many more children to get a higher education." Frank opens with a tempting argument that merits further discussion. Every one of the elders has an opinion on this issue.

"What good would that do them if they can't find suitable employment?" Brother Molrongo is the first to put forth his point of view. He speaks a bit louder than necessary, stabbing the air with his fingers.

"Exposing young children to the ways of the white man is dangerous," Pastor Benadeth offers. I am sure he is thinking of his only daughter, Kwevira, and how reluctant he was to let her leave the island to get a "white man's education."

"Our culture is already in peril. Our ways and the ways of the white governments are not compatible." Bumbu Joshua's voice is quiet, but he commands full attention from everyone. "Who will teach the new generation the ways and customs of their tribes?" Many heads nod.

"Too much choice makes our young children confused and unhappy." Papa Viralongo's voice is calm. He has to consider a big crowd of children and grandchildren. Would he let more of them leave the island for schooling if he had the money? Viralongo fills his shell of kava for the second time.

"We are content with the way things are. Money is not the answer." Uncle Toka gets up to make his views heard. He doesn't seem entirely convinced by his own words, though. Is he imagining living in a house made of concrete? Is he thinking of roads built of asphalt, in which a wagon would not sink in the mud even in the most torrential rain?

The visitors look at each other. Arguments are burning on their tongues, but they are not given a chance to voice them; not until every elder has had a chance to speak.

"We've all heard the sad stories of men from our village who went to work in tourist spots and started running after money. Our people don't know how to resist the temptations of a city. Many started drinking or gambling away their hard-earned salaries. One brother has fathered several children without being married." Paul raises his voice. He has seen these problems first-hand.

The meeting goes on for several hours. Kava flows generously, though I don't touch it. The voices grow quieter and calmer. Then the subject changes to sorcery. The whole village seems gripped with fear; that's why most people have been staying in their huts for the last few days.

"What did you do to our village eldest? Did you not turn into spirits and get into his guts? He fell ill after asking you to leave the village," Uncle Toka wants to know.

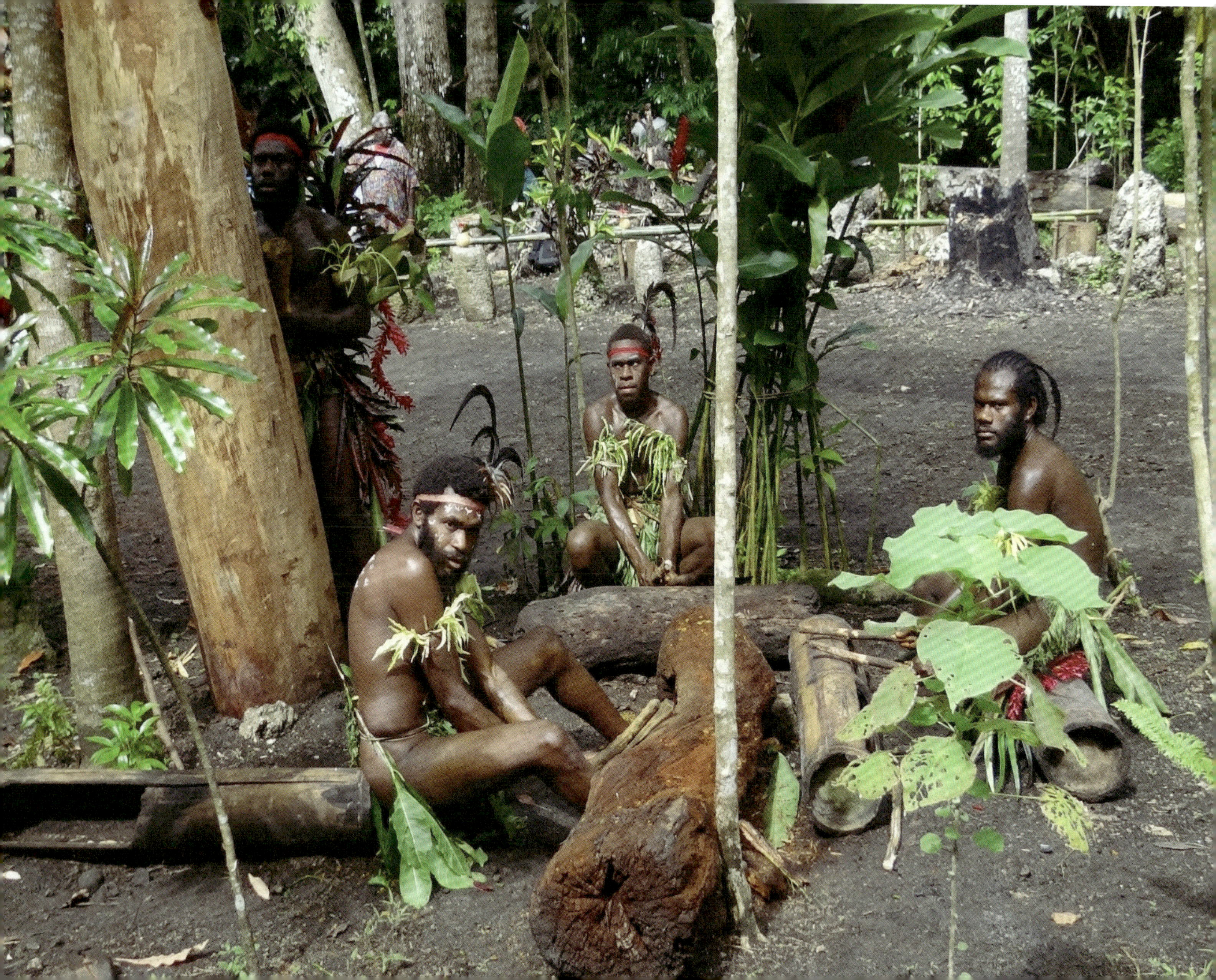

"And what happened to the mango tree? It dropped all its fruit after you passed by," Pastor Benadeth adds without waiting for an answer. He can hardly hide his annoyance. Mangoes are a welcome addition to our meals.

"Too many bad things have occurred since you arrived. What else is going to happen to our people and us if you don't get your way? The pier for the cargo ships almost broke after you arrived. Can you see why we suspect you are using magical powers?" Molrongo's eyes are only half open at this point. Either the kava is getting to him, or he is worn out from the discussions.

"We had nothing to do with it," Lucian assures the group. He looks around the assembly with a big, hopeful smile, which is met with frowns and downcast eyes. He seeks approval from his friends, but they stare straight ahead.

Could there be a different explanation for all these mishaps? I look at Bumbu Joshua and ask him quietly, "Did you feel the devil in your heart because of these men?"

"Dear boy, I have not been very well lately. It may have been the exhaustion and the added strain of their visit. I went to the mountain hut to die, but thanks to you, here I am." A faint smile crosses his thin lips. I grab a shell of kava and hand it to him.

My curiosity is not yet satisfied. I speak quietly, for the nakamal has become silent. A fly buzzes on its way back out the window, and a cloud of gnats dances in the sunlight. I savor sitting here and listening to the birds' calls, feeling my part as one of the men in my community.

"Bumbu Joshua, can mango trees behave in this strange way without magic?" I have never heard that they do, but he would know.

He nods. "That is entirely possible. It can happen because of a change in the underground water supply."

"This actually happens quite frequently," Frank interrupts eagerly. "It was surely not the first time a tree died in your community." He is not comfortable in this situation and keeps combing the hair from his forehead with a jerky motion. I notice a large ring on his index finger. Frank's skin is fairer than any of ours. I wonder what island he is from.

"And your pier was rickety when we arrived." Lucian is now picking up courage. "It was damaged when a wave pushed our boat against it."

With a look towards Frank, Alphonse adds, "We could not help it."

Silence descends again, and kava shells are refilled. Our men are still not convinced that magic was not involved, but I start to see the picture. All three mishaps do have other explanations. As I get up, my legs are shaking slightly, and I hold on to Bumbu Joshua's walking stick to steady my hands. Butterflies in my chest make my voice flutter. The song of the cicadas outside draws attention to the silence inside the nakamal.

I raise my voice, "I learned that there is no power in Black Magic, apart from the power that he, who believes, gives it," I say. My voice trembles a bit, but the words come out clear. I am by far the youngest in the group. Who am I to pass on knowledge to the assembly? My heart beats in my throat, but I keep my gaze high, as all eyes are now on me.

To my surprise, I hear myself say, "This is what I learned about sorcery: it is an idea we resort to when we don't have an explanation for what's happening. Bumbu Joshua assured us that his suffering had nothing to do with you. Lokin has not come to any harm either. Our dog was hiding with him while he was sick. I found the two together." Then I sit down because my knees are shaking. Bumbu Joshua's eyes are resting on me. I can feel he is proud of me. I let my eyes glide from man to man in the circle.

"You don't know the opportunity you are missing. Think of the money, people! Think of the progress this village will make, and everyone in it." Frank speaks his mind clearly, and we hear. He nods to his companions. "Excuse us, we need to talk about this," he says and beckons his friends to follow him outside. All of us stay behind and sit in silence. Everything has been said.

Loud voices tell us of an argument between the three. The village men stay seated; Bumbu Joshua has nodded off. I wonder if I should go out and see what the strangers are up to. Finally, they come back in. "Patrick, the son of Tamar, told us this would be an ideal spot for our business. He's opened a sailing business in Loltong on Pentecost, and says he's rolling in money."

Silence all around. Is everyone still against this or are some of our villagers beginning to waver? I stand up again and clear my throat. "How about we have a show of hands? Who is against the business and all the changes that would come to our way of life?"

Almost all hands shoot into the air. I glance at Bumbu Joshua, whose pipe has fallen to the ground. His eyes are closed, his head is slightly bent forward. It's time to wrap this meeting up.

Uncle Toka sums up the result. "Young men, I think you realize that we do not want your business here. The Lolotitimba people do not want tourists to flood the island." He looks at me.

I get up and say, "Elder Joshua is still in charge. He has decided our village ways, tested and true, should be maintained."

Papa Viralongo ends the discussion by pointing out, "With your brash ways, you frightened everyone." He lets that sink in for a minute. When the men straighten up and make ready to leave the nasara, he adds, "How about you stay a few days and work with us to repair the dock?" Lucien and Alphonse look at Frank. He shrugs. It seems they have nothing urgent to do now and agree to stay and help.

As we make our way back to the village, Bumbu Joshua, in a voice that is almost a whisper, says to the young men by way of encouragement. "Remember that money is a good servant, but a terrible master." He never misses the chance to dispense a few words of wisdom that will guide them in the future. He is exhausted, and I support him by sliding my arm under his.

==//==

Bumbu Joshua did not want to join the family for dinner under the navele tree. I am sitting by his cot in the men's sleeping house, massaging his knees.

"I'm proud of you, my son," Bumbu Joshua says, his words barely audible. I am leaning over him. "You will lead this tribe into the future. You have the gift of keeping unity, and thereby order, in the community. Use it wisely to honor the past while building bridges to the future."

I love what I'm hearing, but I hate what my other senses are telling me. Bumbu Joshua's eyes are almost closed, and his lips make the little smacking sounds I have grown to love. He is barely breathing. Fear grips my stomach, and cold dread makes me shudder. My hands are clutching his as I bring my ears close to his mouth to hear what he might want to say.

A small smile crosses his lips as his eyes close. I am looking for another shallow breath to lift his chest. Nothing… nothing… My own heart begins to throb in my ears. A tear falls from my lashes onto his sunken cheek.

Don't go, Bumbu Joshua, my mind screams. I rest my head on his chest and let my tears flow.

"No, no, no, Bumbu Joshua," I finally wail when I grasp the enormity of what just happened. I stumble blindly towards my father's hut. No words come from my mouth, only cries and sobs. My father understands and takes off running. Bumbu Janet's chin trembles and her shoulders begin to quake. She takes me into her arms. Together we let Bumbu Joshua's spirit know about the grief that is swallowing us.

The news of Bumbu Joshua's death travels up and down the coast like a hurricane. Within a couple of days, relatives from all over the island surge into our village. Many carry a pandanus mat or some colorful cloth to give to Bumbu Janet or to Viralongo and Lovatu. Soon there is not a place left in any of the huts, and newcomers build makeshift shelters for the night.

The air is full of wailing and screaming. Men, women and children are crying, even collapsing in grief. The last of the sun's rays fall with a deep slant onto the men who gathered in the central plaza. Under the shadow of the mango tree, they pound and stomp the ground until their bodies are shaking. Of course, I join them, and I, too, bruise the soft bare ground with my heels, pounding into it all the grief that threatens to crush me. A cloud of dead leaves and dust envelops us. I want to sink into it and stay there, joining Bumbu Joshua on the path he is taking.

For days, nothing will be undertaken; nothing at all will be done. No member of my family will cook a meal, bathe, or clean the village. This way, we can feel and express the sadness of our loss with every fiber of our being. I am grateful to share my grief with so many who loved and revered Bumbu Joshua.

Two of Bumbu Joshua's nephews, as well as the one brother who is still alive, have come to pay their respects. They all want to sleep a night in Bumbu Joshua's cot. They spend hours in his hut; they take turns lounging in his hollowed-out tree trunk; they cradle his beloved pipe.

The evening after three days of such lamentations, every soul that is in our village assembles under the giant banyan tree. In the fading light, everyone comes to rest on a pandanus mat. Cicadas are singing their lullabies. All talk is about Bumbu Joshua, as family and friends are recounting special episodes of his life. When it is almost time to go to our sleeping houses,

Uncle Ruben stands up.

"Joshua, like all great men, had two strong souls," Uncle Ruben draws everyone's gaze to himself. The eyes of the women are red from crying. The men become silent.

"One soul has surely ascended to heaven by now. The other will rest with us. It will continue to help and guide us. Every one of you will, at one time or another, feel his spirit attending or even influencing your actions. Don't be surprised or frightened if this happens."

Not a sound comes from all the people gathered here. Not even the children move. I know from school that man has only one soul, and a dead person does not come back as a ghost. Our pastor has told us as much in one of his Sunday sermons. But is this true for our village, too, where every great leader is said to have two souls? This is rather confusing, but I know now is not the time to dispute a wise elder's pronouncements. I make a note to discuss this further when I'm back in school.

The earthly remains of Bumbu Joshua are buried in a splendid Christian ceremony the following Sunday. Pastor Benadeth's sermon is full of beautiful and comforting words as the gathered mourners say another round of goodbyes and sing some mighty hymns that would have pleased Bumbu Joshua. Soon the moaning of the women turns into crying again, and then the wailing gets so loud that the pastor has to suspend his preaching for several minutes.

The body of Bumbu Joshua, wrapped into red pandanus leaf mats, is lowered into the ground, and everyone passes by to throw a handful of earth onto it. I let my tears flow freely, my sobs mingling with the howling and grieving of the other mourners.

You are in a good place, Bumbu Joshua, a place without pain or swollen knees. I hold his walking stick in my hands. My fingers glide over the smooth knob at its top, as if by magic I could pull Bumbu Joshua's wisdom and courage from it to guide me. *Am I thinking of magic?* I smirk.

I send a short prayer to heaven. *Keep looking after me, will you? I miss you so much.* How thankful I am for having had such a wise and loving Bumbu, and how incomplete I feel without him.

Uncle Toka summons all the men to take their seat under the banyan tree again. I join them as they are chatting with each other, catching up on past events in the visitors' lives. I, too, have no more tears to spend, and I'm interested in events that have taken place several villages down the coast.

I notice with satisfaction that the women are preparing food. Not just food: a feast. I glimpse Kwevira helping her mother. They are sorting out banana leaves. When she sees me, she comes over.

"So sorry you lost your Bumbu Joshua," she says with tears in her beautiful eyes while resting her hand on my forearm.

Nowhere else, with nobody else, doing nothing else but this. Did Bumbu Joshua just speak to me, or did I imagine it? A wave of warmth spreads from my stomach and into every limb. Kwevira's words and gentle touch comfort me. I smile at her and know that the upcoming trip back to school will be a good one. Together we will find out what part of our education will benefit our tribe in the future.

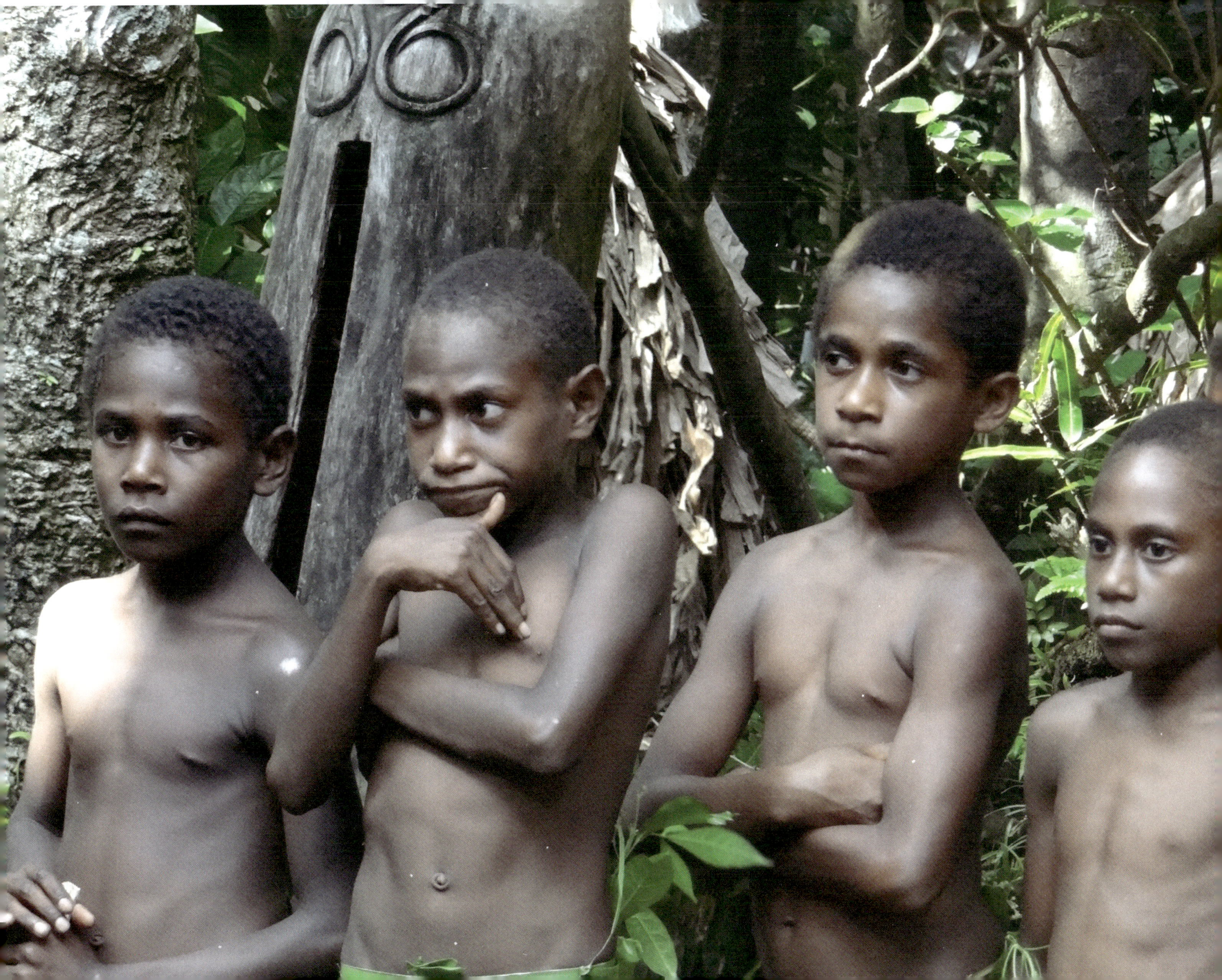

POINTS TO CONSIDER:

Vanuatu is home to 250,000 inhabitants, organized in tribes and clans who speak 105 different languages. Bislama, a kind of pidgin English, serves as a native tongue.

When the people of Vanuatu embraced Christianity, tribal wars came to an end. The church forbade pig killing ceremonies and all forms of sorcery. There was a period when the people became unsure of where the power lay, but they learned to take their cues from the church.

Traditional Nakamals

In north and central Vanuatu, the nakamal generally takes the form of a large building, assembled from traditional materials. Under the direction of a particular chief, the entire community helps to build such a structure. Entry to the nakamal is usually restricted to men, and the building may be used as a sleeping and living area for unmarried men and boys as well as for male visitors to the village. Significantly, most nakamals lack a lockable door, indicating that all friendly visitors are welcome, although there may be a low barrier across the entrance to keep out animals. In front of a nakamal there is often a flattened clearing, or nasara, used for dances and outdoor gatherings.

A Chief is recognized as the uppermost figure in a community. The Vanuatu Council of Chiefs, "Malvatumauri," is recognized by the constitution of the Republic of Vanuatu. The chief system in Vanuatu has a long history of community matters being settled by tribal village chiefs.

https://blogs.adb.org/blog/mobilize-communities-vanuatu-talk-chiefs

Abel thanks you for reading the story of his childhood on his beloved island of Ambae. After he graduated from Ranwadi High, he was awarded a scholarship to attend college in Port Vila. After this, he attended the University of the South Pacific in Suva, Fiji.

Abel did become a teacher on Ambrym, where he met and married an Australian volunteer teacher, Kathy. Later, he went on to work for the Vanuatu Rural Development Training Centers' Association. For three years he headed the Ministry of Agriculture, Forestry and Fisheries. From there he transferred to the highest public service post, filling the position of Director General of Education.

With the sale of this book, Abel and Kathy have so far financed two 1000 liter water tanks for schools in Vanuatu.

If you'd like to discover more of Vanuatu, contact:
trekvanuatu.com.au

TREK Vanuatu
Tour Rural Endangered Kalja

Learn the language of Bislama:

https://www.vanuatu.travel/en/local-knowledge/local-knowledge-learn-bislama

Vanuatu's National Anthem

Original Bislama Version

Yumi, Yumi, Yumi
Glad blong talem se:
Yumi, Yumi, Yumi
Man blong Vanuatu.

God i givim ples ia long yumi,
Yumi glad tumas long hem,
Yumi strong mo yumi fri long hem,
Yumi brata evriwan.

Plante fasin blong bifo i stap,
Plante fasin blong tedei,
Be yumi i olsem wan nomo,
Hemia fasin blong yumi.

Yumi save plante wok i stap,
Long ol aelan blong yumi,
God i helpem yumi evriwan,
Hemi papa blong yumi

Anglicised Version

You-me, you-me, you-me
Glad belong tell'em say:
You-me, you-me, you-me
Man belong Vanuatu.

God ee give'm place here along you-me
You-me glad too-much along him
You-me strong more you-me free along him
You-me brother everyone.

Plenty fashion belong before ee stop
Plenty fashion belong today
But you-me ee all-same one no-more
Him-here fashion belong you-me.

You-me savvy plenty work ee stop
Along all island belong you-me
God ee help'em you-me everyone
Him-here papa belong you-me.

English Translation

We, we, we
Are happy to say:
We, we, we
Are the people of Vanuatu!

God has given us this place,
We are very glad of this,
We are strong and we are free here,
We are all brothers.

Many old traditions remain,
and many new ones come.
But we are one people,
That is our way.

We know there is much work to be done
On our islands,
God helps us all,
He is our father.

MY SINCERE THANKS GO TO:

Abel Nako, who not only indulged my curiosity during our three trips to Vanuatu, but kept sending me memories of his childhood, despite his busy lifestyle. Thanks also to Kathy for filling in when Abel was not available.

Raul Touzon, a National Geographic Photographer, who kindly shared his spectacular photos with me. The center spreads, the picture on page 26, 59 & 87 and the back cover are products of his camera and skill.

Martin Naughton, who thought the story was good enough to be reading material for schools in Ireland. Thanks for the encouragement and deadline.

Laura Burge, my editor, for her questions and suggestions. She combed through every line of this manuscript as if she wanted to learn it by heart.

And my husband Mike, for his precious input and his patience, his pictures and his good advice.

CPSIA information can be obtained at www.ICGtesting.com
Printed in the USA
BVIW121553030220
571271BV00013B/135